Geography

THE STUDY OF SCIENCE

Geography

Edited by Jason Shattuck

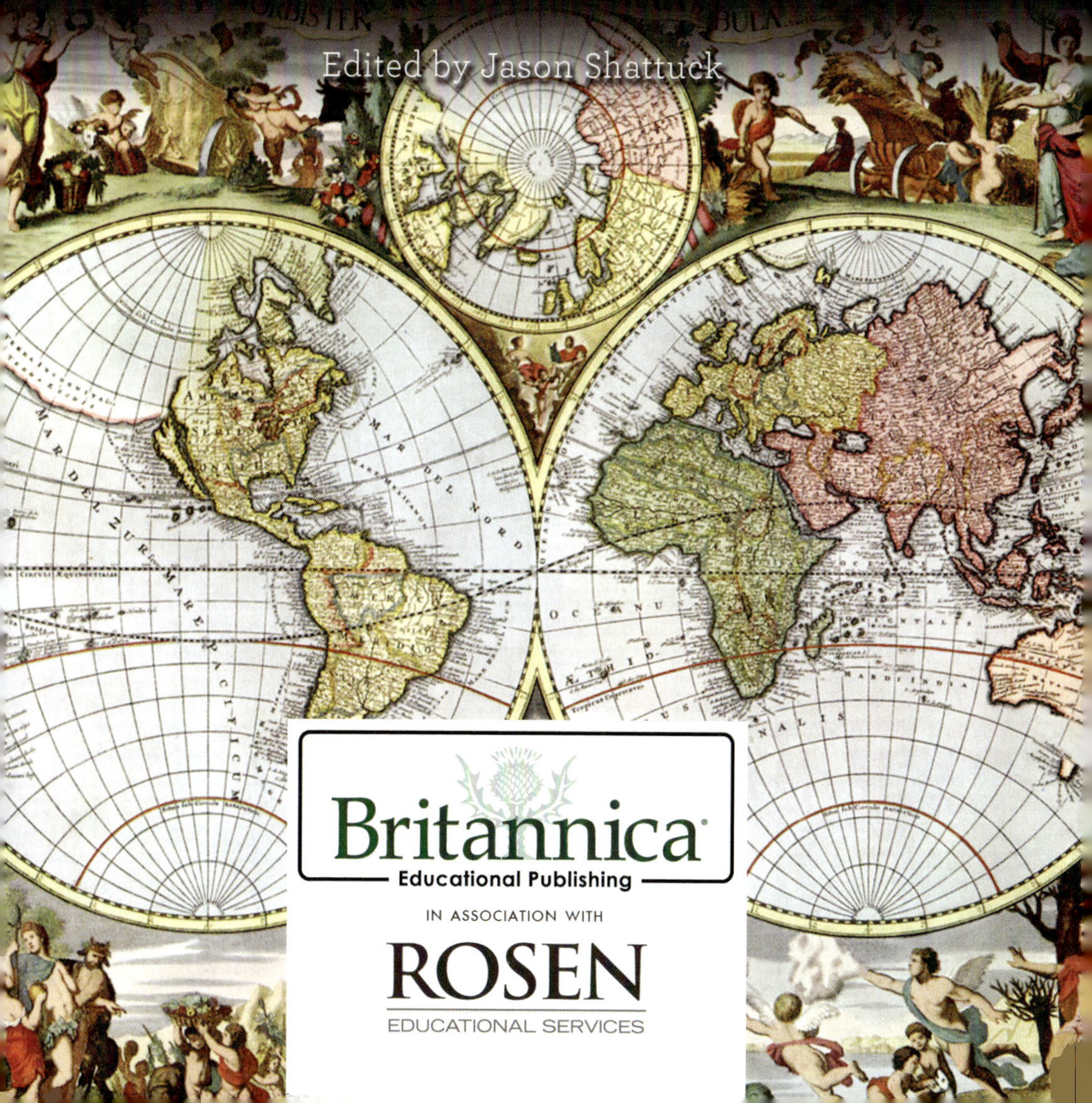

Britannica Educational Publishing

IN ASSOCIATION WITH

ROSEN EDUCATIONAL SERVICES

Published in 2017 by Britannica Educational Publishing (a trademark of Encyclopædia Britannica, Inc.) in association with The Rosen Publishing Group, Inc.
29 East 21st Street, New York, NY 10010

Distributed exclusively by Rosen Publishing.
To see additional Britannica Educational Publishing titles, go to rosenpublishing.com.

First Edition

Britannica Educational Publishing
J.E. Luebering: Executive Director, Core Editorial
Anthony L. Green: Editor, Compton's by Britannica

Rosen Publishing
Kathy Kuhtz Campbell: Senior Editor
Nelson Sá: Art Director
Brian Garvey: Designer
Cindy Reiman: Photography Manager
Nicole DiMella: Photo Researcher
Supplementary text by Jason Shattuck

Library of Congress Cataloging-in-Publication Data

Names: Shattuck, Jason, editor.
Title: Geography / edited by Jason Shattuck.
Description: New York, NY : Britannica Educational Publishing in association with the Rosen Educational Services, Inc., 2017. | Series: The study of science | Includes bibliographical references and index.
Identifiers: LCCN 2016020436 | ISBN 9781508104285 (library bound)
Subjects: LCSH: Geography—Juvenile literature.
Classification: LCC G133 .G47 2017 | DDC 910—dc23
LC record available at https://lccn.loc.gov/2016020436

Manufactured in China

Photo credits: Cover, p. 3 Culture Club/Hulton Archive/Getty Images; pp. 8–9 Wolfgang Kaehler/LightRocket/Getty Images; pp. 13, 17, 18, 46, 56, 71, 72 Encyclopædia Britannica, Inc.; p. 21 NASA GSFC; p. 23 Chaput Franck/Hemis.fr/Getty Images; p. 25 U.S. Geological Survey/photo by Jonathan Godt; p. 27 Eye Ubiquitous/SuperStock; p. 28 © Dr. Morley Read/Shutterstock.com; p. 29 Janelle Lugge/Shutterstock.com; p. 31 Rosemary Calvert/Photographer's Choice/Getty Images; p. 35 Graham Crouch/Lonely Planet Images/Getty Images; p. 37 Ray Manley/Shostal Associates; p. 41 © Robert Frerck/Odyssey Productions; p. 43 Cotton Coulson/National Geographic Image Collection/Getty Images; p. 50 DEA/M. Santini/De Agostini/Getty Images; p. 57 Ali Zifan/Wikimedia/File:Countries by GDP (PPP) Per Capita in 2014.svg/CC0 1.0; p. 59 Library of Congress Geography and Map Division; p. 62 DEA/G. Dagli Orti/De Agostini/Getty Images; p. 64 Texas Parks and Wildlife GIS Lab; p. 68 © iStockphoto.com/Pamela Moore; p. 69 gallimaufry/Shutterstock.com; p. 75 steve estvanik/Shutterstock.com; p. 81 © 2011 MapQuest; p. 91 Hulton Archive/Getty Images; p. 94 ullstein bild/Getty Images; p. 99 © AP Images; cover and interior pages backgrounds and borders © iStockphoto.com/LuMaxArt.

CONTENTS

INTRODUCTION

Mount Rainier, part of the Cascade Range, and Eunice Lake, which was carved by glaciers, are located in Washington State. They are surrounded by meadows and forested land.

As the study of the diverse environments, places, and spaces of Earth's surface, geography seeks to answer the questions of why things are as they are, where they are. The modern academic discipline of geography is rooted in ancient practice, concerned with the characteristics of places, in particular their natural environments and peoples, as well as the interrelations between the two. Its separate identity as a discipline was first formulated and named some two thousand years ago by the Greeks, whose *geo* and *graphein* were combined to mean "earth writing" or "earth description." However, what people now understand as geography was elaborated before then, in the Arab world and elsewhere. Ptolemy, author of one of the discipline's first books, *Guide to Geography* (second century CE), defined geography as "a representation in pictures of the whole known world together with the phenomena which are contained therein." This expresses what many still consider geography's essence—a description of the world using maps (and now also pictures, as in the kind of popular geography exemplified by *National Geographic Magazine*, a monthly magazine of geography, archaeology, anthropology, and exploration). However, as more was learned about the world, the study of geography acquired a more scientific approach.

To most people, geography means knowing where places are and what they are like. Discussion of an area's geography usually refers to its topography—its relief and drainage patterns and predominant vegetation, along with climate and weather patterns—together with human responses to that environment, as in agricultural, industrial, and other land uses and in settlement and urbanization patterns.

Although there was a much earlier teaching of what is now called geography, the academic discipline is largely a twentieth-century creation, forming a bridge between the natural and social sciences. The history of geography is the history of thinking about the concepts of environments, places, and spaces. Its content covers an understanding of the physical spaces humans occupy, as well as our transformations of environments into places that we find more comfortable to inhabit (though many modifications have negative impacts). Geography provides insights into major contemporary issues, such as globalization and environmental change, as well as a detailed appreciation of local differences.

Geographers are interested in Earth's physical features—mountains, deserts, rivers, oceans, rocks, and minerals—and in the ways that people affect and are affected by the natural world. Physical geographers examine, measure, and describe Earth's surface and study how landforms develop and change, and how different landforms influence climate. They also investigate how people transform the land through their activities, such as erecting cities, digging mines, and clearing forests. Human geographers focus on where people live, what they do, and how they utilize the land. They might study why urban areas develop in specific places and what the cultures of different peoples are like, including customs, languages, and religions.

In this reference, readers consider a general review of geography, the natural and human elements that make up the physical world, and how these are studied within the discipline.

CHAPTER 1

AN OVERVIEW OF GEOGRAPHY

The field of geography can be broadly divided into two areas of study: physical geography and human geography. Physical geography is concerned with places. Human geography is concerned with the people in the places—how and why they live where they do, and how their social, economic, and cultural characteristics vary from one place to another. This chapter and chapter 2 focus on the main areas of interest to physical geographers. The concerns of human geography are addressed in chapter 3.

A key aspect of the planet's surface that geographers study is the variability of the environment from place to place. Have you ever observed your hometown from a point of land or building high enough to see all or much of it at one time? If you have, you undoubtedly noticed that it is composed of areas or parts that differ from one another in rather striking ways. Perhaps one part is high and dry, another low and wet. Most of the land occupied by your community may be used for homes, but these probably also differ from section to section. In one section of your community, the houses may be large, expensive, and widely spaced. In another, they may be small, less costly, and built close together. Some buildings may be single-family dwellings.

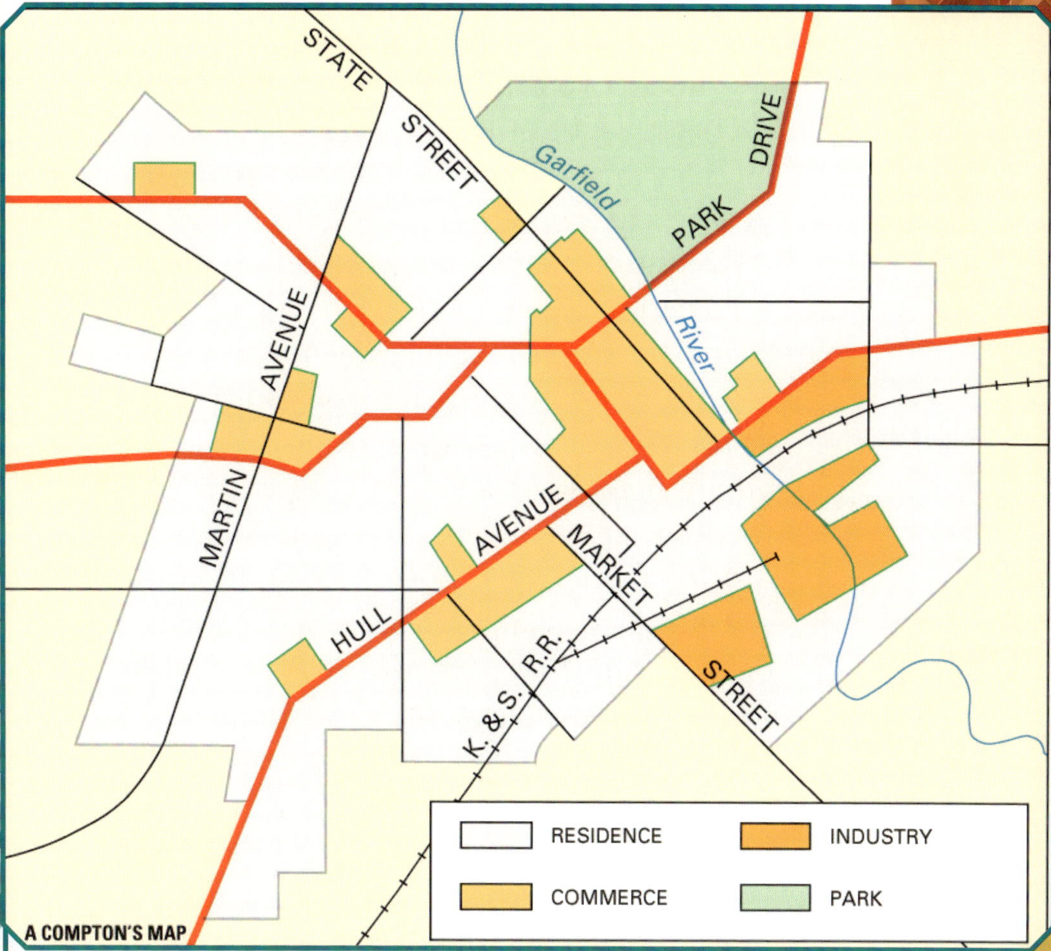

A study of a town's pattern reveals associations between different parts. Factories are apt to be near railroads. Stores stand on busy streets and where bus lines intersect.

Others may be tall apartment buildings providing homes for hundreds of families.

A study of your community will show that there is a pattern in the location of certain things. For example, you will likely find that factories are generally associated with railroads and that more expensive homes occupy the higher and drier pieces of land. You will probably see that the shopping areas are located where routes of transportation converge. You will likely notice too that the large apartment buildings are generally placed nearer the business centers than are the single-family homes.

If you continue your study, you will also find that each part of your community is connected with all of the others in some way. You will see that there is a continuous flow of goods and people back and forth.

You are making observations regarding (1) the distribution of things within your community; (2) the association in space of different things and places; and (3) the flow of goods and people from one part of the community to another. As you make these observations, you are studying the geography of your local community.

If you could observe the distribution of things over the face of Earth from high above its surface, you would notice other differences

Geography as a Social Science

Any discipline or branch of science that deals with the social and cultural aspects of human behavior can be called a social science. Among the disciplines comprising the social sciences are economics, psychology, sociology, geography, and political science.

With aspects of physical as well as social science, geography is the study of the features of Earth's surface and of their relationships to each other and to humankind. This study encompasses several subfields. Physical geography incorporates some earth sciences such as climatology, hydrography, and geomorphology, the study of landforms. Human geography involves the economic, political, and social activities of people in communities and cultures. Historical geography examines the geography of past historical periods. Another area of geography is cartography, the recording of geographic facts in the form of maps. The structure and dynamics of human populations, including age, sex, births, deaths, and migratory movements, are investigated in the field of demography.

from place to place. You would see differences in the distribution of natural objects and of works made by people. You would observe that certain things occur together, just as some things were associated in your home community.

You would also note that there is a constant flow of goods and people from one part of Earth to another. As you examine these facts, you are studying geography on a global scale. In a like manner, you can study the geography of any part of Earth's surface, such as the geography of Asia, of the United States, or of the midwestern region of the United States.

By now you may have inferred that the study of geography incorporates two very basic and important considerations: the location of specific places or things, and the patterns formed by the distribution of these entities over Earth.

LOCATION

If you were asked to find the location of a house or a store within your local community, you could do it easily. You would simply look up its address; that is, its street and number.

Similarly, a system of addresses is used to help locate places on Earth's surface. This numbering system is based on two imaginary lines—the equator and the prime meridian. Distances in degrees north or south of the equator measure latitude. Distances in degrees east or west of the prime meridian measure longitude.

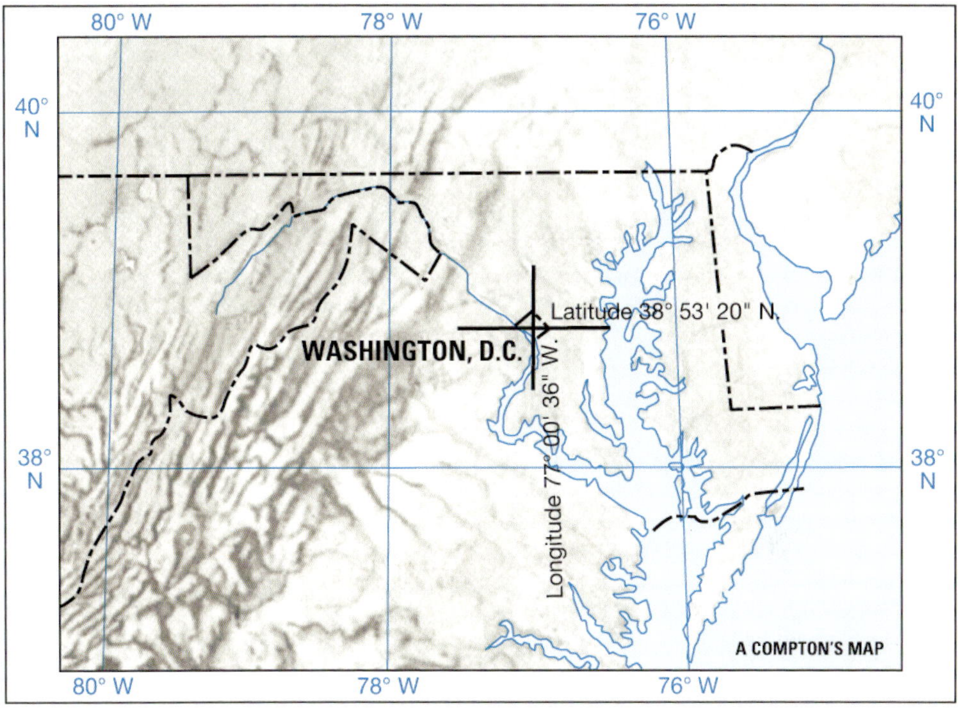

To find the exact location of a place, such as Washington, DC, one must use a map that shows latitude and longitude. No two places have the same exact location.

Together, the latitude and longitude of a place provides its exact location—its geographic address. For example, the exact location of Washington, DC, may be given as 38° 53′ 20″ north latitude and 77° 00′ 36″ west longitude. No other place on Earth's surface has this same latitude and longitude, just as no other place in your hometown has the same address you do.

Washington, DC, may be located in relation to many natural and political features on this map. It is on the Potomac River, east of the Appalachians, and southwest of Baltimore and Philadelphia.

The location of a place can also be given by noting its position in relation to something else. For example, the site of your home community can be given in terms of its distance and direction with respect to another city or to some river, railroad, or major highway. This type of location is known as relative location.

A third way of locating a place is in terms of its natural setting. New York City is situated along the Atlantic coast; Nevada is in the Great Basin; and La Paz, Bolivia, is in the Andes Mountains. This is referred to as the natural location of a place.

PATTERNS

To study geography, one first must be able to locate specific things or places. Geography also deals with the arrangement of similar types of things over the face of Earth. Three different kinds of patterns are generally studied: patterns of points, patterns of lines, and patterns of areas.

Examining the distribution of villages, towns, or cities over Earth's surface, one observes patterns of points. These occupy small areas and appear on maps as dots. On the other hand, some things form continuous lines. Rivers, political boundaries, railroads, and roads are examples of things that make patterns of lines. Mountain systems, different kinds of farming, or different classes of soils form patterns of areas. The study of geography is concerned with the description and explanation of these three types of patterns on the face of Earth.

CHAPTER 2

PATTERNS OF NATURAL ELEMENTS

Physical geography investigates natural features and how physical processes formed Earth's surface. The elements of the physical world with which geography is concerned include all the objects that are seen when Earth itself is examined. These objects number in the millions, but they can be grouped into classes—the major classes include continents and oceans, landforms, weather and climate, rocks and minerals, Earth's waters, and plants and animals.

CONTINENTS AND OCEANS

The continents are the large masses of land that stand above the level of the seas. There are seven continents—Asia, Africa, North America, South America, Antarctica, Europe, and Australia, listed in order of size. (Europe and Asia are sometimes considered a single continent,

North and South America are shown as they might appear from space at a point 22,000 miles (35,000 kilometers) above Earth. Data from two satellites (one collecting land data, the other gathering cloud data) were combined to make this image.

Eurasia.) Together the continents cover about 29 percent of Earth's surface.

A world globe shows that there is twice as much land in the Northern Hemisphere as there is south of the equator. The major landmasses of the north form an almost complete belt around the Arctic Ocean, leaving only three outlets to other bodies of water. The North Pole, which represents the northern end of Earth's axis, lies in the Arctic Ocean, about 450 miles (725 kilometers) north of Greenland. At the southern tip of Earth's axis, the South Pole presents a different picture. It is located near the center of the frozen continent of Antarctica.

The oceans comprise a large continuous body of water that is broken into irregular parts by continents and islands. Most researchers recognize five major oceans—the Pacific, Atlantic, Indian, Arctic, and Southern, or Antarctic. Together with their gulfs, bays, and seas, the oceans cover about 71 percent of Earth's surface.

LANDFORMS

Earth's surface can be broadly described as being rough or smooth. The rough lands include the world's mountains and hilly uplands. The smooth, or flat, lands are its plateaus and plains.

Each continent has its particular arrangement of landforms, though similarities do exist. For example, high mountain ranges are located along the western sides of both North and South America, since the two continents essentially compose one landmass. Each also has older and relatively smaller mountains near its eastern borders. Wide plains drained by great river systems fill the spaces between the mountain masses. Both continents have narrow coastal plains along their western margins and wider plains in the east.

Eurasia (Europe and Asia combined) and Africa differ remarkably from North and South America in their surfaces. A long mountain

Grootberg Plateau is part of the wide, flat Central Plateau in the Kunene region of Namibia in Africa. The Central Plateau, which extends over half of Namibia and runs from north to south, is where most of the country's people live.

axis extends across south-central Eurasia. To the north and northwest of this mountain core lies the largest lowland in the world, stretching from the Atlantic Ocean far into Asia.

Geomorphology: The Description and Classification of Landforms

Geomorphology is the scientific discipline concerned with the description and classification of Earth's topographic features. (Topography is the configuration of features such as mountains and rivers in an area of land. It is also the art or science of making maps that show the height, shape, and similar features of the land in a particular area.)

Much geomorphologic research has been devoted to the origin of landforms. Such studies focus on the forces that mold and alter the primary relief elements of the terrestrial surface. These forces include tectonic activity and surface movements (for example, landslides and rockfalls). They also involve weathering and the erosion and deposition of the resulting rock debris by wind, glacial ice, and streams. In recent years, increasing attention has been given to the effects of human action on the physical environment as well.

Some systems of classifying landforms describe and group topographic features primarily based on the processes that shaped or modified them. Others consider additional factors, such as the character of the surface rocks and

On March 22, 2014, a perilous hillside above Oso, Washington, collapsed, spilling mud, rocks, and timber onto the neighborhood below. The landslide killed forty-three people. Scientists believe it was caused partly by saturating rainfall over a forty-five-day period .

climatic variations, and include the developmental stage of landforms as an aspect of their evolution over geologic time.

Geomorphology is closely allied with a number of other scientific disciplines that are concerned with natural processes. Fluvial (river-related) and coastal geomorphology rely heavily on fluid mechanics and sedimentology. Studies of mass movement, weathering, wind action, and soils draw on the atmospheric and soil sciences. Research on certain landform types entails the principles and methods of geophysics and volcanology. The study of the human impact upon landforms relies on the disciplines of geography and human ecology.

Africa is not nearly as mountainous as Asia. With the exception of the Atlas Mountains in the northwest, the highest mountains are in the east-central part of Africa. Most of inner Africa is a vast plateau, greatly cut and worn by rivers to form a hilly region.

Australia has three dominant landforms. They are the highlands in the east, the plateaus in the west, and a vast plains area covering the east-central part of the continent. Antarctica is a mountainous land that has many ranges and peaks.

ROCKS AND MINERALS

There are several thousand known types of minerals, about 100 of which constitute the major mineral components of rocks; these are the so-called rock-forming minerals.

Minerals are unequally distributed over the face of Earth. Some countries and continents have large supplies of certain valuable minerals; others have little. For example, the largest tin deposits are found in East Asian countries, notably China, Thailand, and Indonesia; Bolivia, Brazil, Great Britain and Russia also have sizeable deposits. In contrast, tin is not found to any significant degree in North America.

A miner digs in a tin mine in Potosí, Bolivia. Mining is Bolivia's leading industry. The country exports zinc, tin, silver, lead, and gold, among other minerals.

Weather and Climate

The conditions of the atmosphere that determine an area's weather include temperature, precipitation (rain and snow), atmospheric pressure, winds, humidity, and percentage of cloudiness and sunshine. The combination of

This stream in the Amazon rainforest is located in Ecuador. The Amazon rainforest has a tropical climate, with vast amounts of rainfall, very high humidity, and exceedingly high temperatures.

these conditions over a period of many years make up an area's climate.

Because the combination of climatic conditions differs from place to place, geography is concerned with the classification of areas according to climate. Areas that have heavy rainfall throughout the year, with average temperatures usually above 80°F (27°C) and average annual temperature ranges of generally not more than 5 or 6°F (about 3°C), have a rainy tropical climate. The Amazon Basin, the Congo Basin, and Indonesia are among the areas that have these climatic conditions.

The arrangement of places having similar climate is fairly regular over Earth's surface. For example, areas with a Mediterranean

The Simpson Desert in central Australia has red sand dunes or ridges. The desert's climate is extremely dry, with most parts receiving 5 inches (125 millimeters) of precipitation or less each year.

climate (hot dry summers and cool moist winters) occur on the west coasts of continents between about 30° and 45° latitude north and south of the equator.

EARTH'S WATERS

Water—especially fresh water—varies from place to place in amount and in other ways, such as purity, odor, and hardness. In some parts of the world, the water supply is almost poisonous because of its great salt content. In other places, it has an unpleasant odor because of the dissolved minerals it contains.

Not all parts of the world have abundant fresh water with the qualities desired. In deserts or semiarid lands, it may be difficult to find enough fresh water to meet the daily requirements of the human population, as well as for the plants and animals that sustain the latter. Large cities, even in humid areas, also have serious supply problems. The distribution of fresh water has become an increasingly important aspect of geographic inquiry.

PLANTS AND ANIMALS

Plants, animals, and all of the living things that inhabit an ecosystem (everything that exists in

A split view of one of the atolls in the Maldives displays the beach with palm trees and the fish and coral reef within the ocean. The Maldives atolls have a biologically diverse ecosystem.

BIOGEOGRAPHY

Biogeography is the study of the geographic distribution of plants and animals. It is concerned not only with habitation patterns but also with the factors responsible for variations in distribution. Strictly speaking, biogeography is a branch of biology, but physical geographers have made important contributions, particularly in the study of flora.

Biogeographic studies divide Earth's surface—primarily the continents and islands—into regions exhibiting differences in the average composition of flora and fauna. It is thought that the present-day distribution patterns of plant and animal forms, as reflected in such biogeographic regions, are the result of many historical and current causes. These causes include present climatic and geographic conditions, the geologic history of the landmasses and their climates, and the evolution of the taxon (for example, genus or species) involved. Investigators have found that rate of dispersal, adaptability to prevailing environmental conditions, and the age of the taxa being studied also have a significant impact on pattern and extent of distribution.

a particular environment), comprise the biotic factors of geography. The field of geography also studies the interaction of these living organisms with the elements and processes of the physical Earth and the resulting effects on ecosystems.

Natural vegetation and animal life vary according to temperature, rainfall, soil, land surface, and other conditions. Together, these factors comprise a life zone, or biome. Because vegetation is usually the dominant and most apparent feature of the landscape, a biome is characterized by its plant community. The four chief biomes are forests, grasslands, deserts, and tundras. Forests are commonly found where the climate is humid and not too cold for trees to grow. Grasslands generally develop in subhumid or semiarid regions where the rainfall is less than that necessary for trees. Deserts occur in places where rainfall is so scarce that even grass has difficulty growing. Tundras are found where the climate is cool to cold throughout the year.

Each type of biome is associated with certain species of animal life. Tropical rainforests, for example, grow in the warm wetlands near the equator. Insects, snakes, and tree-dwelling animals such as birds and monkeys are associated with this type of forest.

Chapter 3

Patterns of Human Elements

Human geography is concerned with the global distribution of people—the ways in which they are arranged and the activities they engage in. These elements may number in the millions but can be grouped into five major categories. The first four—social, economic, cultural, and political—largely reflect the main areas of contemporary life (that is, where and how people live, and the influences of political and other factors on settlement patterns and interactions), and form the main focus of this chapter. The fifth category, historical geography, is addressed in chapter 4.

Where People Live

The majority of the people of the world live on only 10 percent of Earth's surface. This uneven distribution of the world's people is one of the most significant facts of geography. In contrast to the large areas of

Takeshita Street is a pedestrian-only thoroughfare in the Harajuku district of Tokyo, Japan. Tokyo is ranked as the largest city in the world in population, with about 13.4 million people.

uninhabited and sparsely inhabited portions of Earth, the four most densely populated areas are: (1) Southeast Asia, eastern China, Korea, and Japan; (2) the subcontinent of India, Pakistan, Sri Lanka, Bangladesh, and coastal Myanmar; (3) western and central Europe; and (4) the northeastern United States and a small part of neighboring Canada. Among the sparsely populated areas are the polar lands; the deserts; the hot, humid Amazon basin; and the barren highlands of inner Asia.

Differences exist from place to place in the physical characteristics of various groups of people. There are also differences in the languages spoken, the levels of education, the art and music created, and the tools and techniques used to carry out human activities.

DIFFERENCES IN HOUSING

Differences in shelter, or housing, are easily recognizable by the student of geography and by the traveler interested in where things occur on Earth. These differences result from a range of factors, such as available materials, the suitability of those materials to local climate and related conditions, cultural

The apartment-style adobe buildings at Taos Pueblo in New Mexico are typical of the architecture built by the Pueblo Indians. Adobe is a mixture of clay, sand, and silt.

preferences, and the amount and cost of space on which to build.

In the United States, frame houses are abundant in areas where vast forests provided plentiful supplies of lumber. The Native Americans of the arid Southwest use sun-dried brick for their adobe houses and pueblos. Early settlers in the nearly treeless Great Plains lived in sod houses until they could buy and transport lumber. Around the world even more striking contrasts appear. The nomadic

ADOBE

A Spanish word for sun-dried clay bricks, *adobe* also refers to structures built from such bricks and to the clay soil from which the bricks are made. The use of adobe dates back thousands of years in several parts of the world, especially in areas with arid or semiarid climates.

Adobe bricks are usually made by wetting a quantity of suitable soil and allowing it to stand for a day or more in order to soften. A small amount of straw or other fibrous material is then added to the soil. These materials are mixed with a hoe and trampled upon with bare feet. Then the adobe is poured into simple lumber or sheet-metal molds that have four sides and are open at the top and bottom. The bricks are laid out to dry in the sun and are turned from day to day so that they dry evenly. Then they are stacked up under cover until needed. The bricks vary in size—in width and length as well as thickness—depending on their intended use. In the brick-making industry, assembly-line techniques are used to manufacture adobe bricks.

In dry climates, adobe is an excellent building material. With proper care and construction, adobe structures may last for centuries. Adobe is inexpensive and can be produced in abundance in regions where there is clay soil. The art of building with adobe was undoubtedly brought to Spain from northern Africa and then to the New World by the Spanish. American Indians in the southwestern United States built walls by hand, manipulating the pliable clay into courses, or layers, and allowing each course to dry before adding each subsequent layer.

Adobe structures have remarkable insulation properties, allowing their interiors to stay evenly warm in winter and cool in summer. To protect them against heavy or frequent

rains, adobe walls are usually built on solid waterproof foundations of stone or concrete. This practice prevents the action of groundwater from causing any disintegration of the lower layers, which are set in a mortar of the same material. These bricks are finished with a coat of adobe, or sometimes with lime or cement plaster.

peoples of Central Asia, for example, live in tentlike dwellings called yurts. These are large dwellings erected on wooden poles and covered with skin, felt, or handwoven textiles in bright colors. Houses in the small villages of many west African countries may include traditional round mud huts with thatched roofs that maximize air circulation. Housing in large cities around the world may reflect a range of styles, from small brick dwellings to large, modern high-rise dwellings.

Differences in Work

All over the world people work for a living. The global human population performs hundreds, perhaps thousands, of different kinds of jobs. In general, the chief concern is the production of food, clothing, shelter, and tools. The study of geography includes the distribution over Earth's surface of the principal occupations of humankind—fishing, hunting, mining, grazing, lumbering, farming, manufacturing, commerce, and technology.

AGRICULTURE

A large part of Earth's land is used for agriculture. There are many different kinds of farms. They may be grouped into types according to five criteria: (1) crops and livestock produced; (2) farming methods; (3) intensity of the farm operations; (4) disposal of the product; and (5) buildings necessary to house the farm family and farm operations. For example, dairy farming is common throughout most of Wisconsin. The principal livestock are dairy cattle, but hogs and chickens are also raised. Hay, corn (maize) for silage, and oats are the principal crops. Farming methods are highly mechanized, even to the milking of the cows. The fields are well fertilized. Most farmers rotate their crops from year to year and practice recommended measures of soil conservation. Cattle barns are large, and nearby are huge silos and a milkhouse facility. If the operation is a family farm, it will include housing for family members. The milk and milk products are produced for sale at market

Holstein-Friesian cows graze in the pasture of a Wisconsin dairy farm. Dairying encompasses the breeding, raising, and utilization of dairy animals, mostly cows, for the production of milk and the dairy products processed from it.

rather than for consumption by the farmers. Dairy farming, therefore, is a commercial type of farming.

Other types of commercial farming, such as grain farming, mixed farming, and horticulture, are practiced in different parts of the United States and of the world. Some commercial farms are large enterprises run by vast organizations; other commercial farms are relatively small family-based farms. In contrast are small farms that are more subsistent than commercial.

Lands used for grazing offer contrasts with cultivated lands. Generally grazing lands are too rough for the plow, or the climate is too cold or too dry for crops. Grazing lands and practices differ from one another also. Cattle ranching in northern Mexico, for example, has little in common with reindeer grazing overseen by the Sami (Lapps) of Norway.

MINING, LOGGING, AND OTHER INDUSTRIES

Where Earth yields valuable minerals, people find it profitable to use the land for mining. Contrasting types of mining include the open pits of the Lake Superior iron ranges, the bituminous coal mines in the Appalachian fields, and placer mining for tin in Southeast Asia.

People engage in logging and lumbering where they find forested land—provided, of course, that they can transport the logs and lumber to market at a profit. Lumbering methods differ. Logging of great Douglas firs in the Pacific Northwest calls for methods different from those used in cutting pulpwood in Canada or in the pine forests of the southern United States.

Thousands of different manufacturing industries are scattered over the world. They

Workers herd Douglas fir logs at a sawmill in Coos Bay, Oregon, in the late 1970s. In the 1900s, several industries developed around the port at Coos Bay, including shipbuilding and lumber.

vary from handicrafts, such as basketmaking, and simple processing of raw materials, such as canning fruits, to complex operations calling for skilled workmanship and intricate machinery.

Geographers study the conditions that lead the people of a given area to specialize in a certain occupation. For instance, geographers may study the general location of the iron and steel industry in a particular city, state, or country and try to explain why it is there.

ARRANGEMENTS OF POLITICAL UNITS

Political maps show the distribution of governmental units: independent states and colonies or other types of dependencies. Some governmental units occupy relatively large areas; others are small. The geographer is interested in a country's size and shape and in its location—exact, relative, and natural. Of special interest is the location of a country relative to other countries and to mineral resources, trade routes, and similar factors.

The boundaries and core areas of governmental units are also of critical interest to geographers. Core areas are those parts of a country that are most densely populated. Often these are the regions of greatest economic development, such as the Paris basin of France and the manufacturing belt of the northeastern United States.

The study of governmental units also includes an analysis of the character of the country itself. This involves the ability of the country to support its people; the differences among places within the country; and the country's capacity to become a world power.

Settlement Patterns

In order to carry on their different activities, people have established themselves in various ways on Earth's surface. Some live in temporary settlements and travel about. Most people, however, live in more permanent settlements. Geography is concerned with the character and patterns of both rural and urban settlements.

Rural settlements are those that are related to farming, lumbering, mining, fishing, and hunting. In some places, people engaged in these activities live separately from one another. For instance, in some

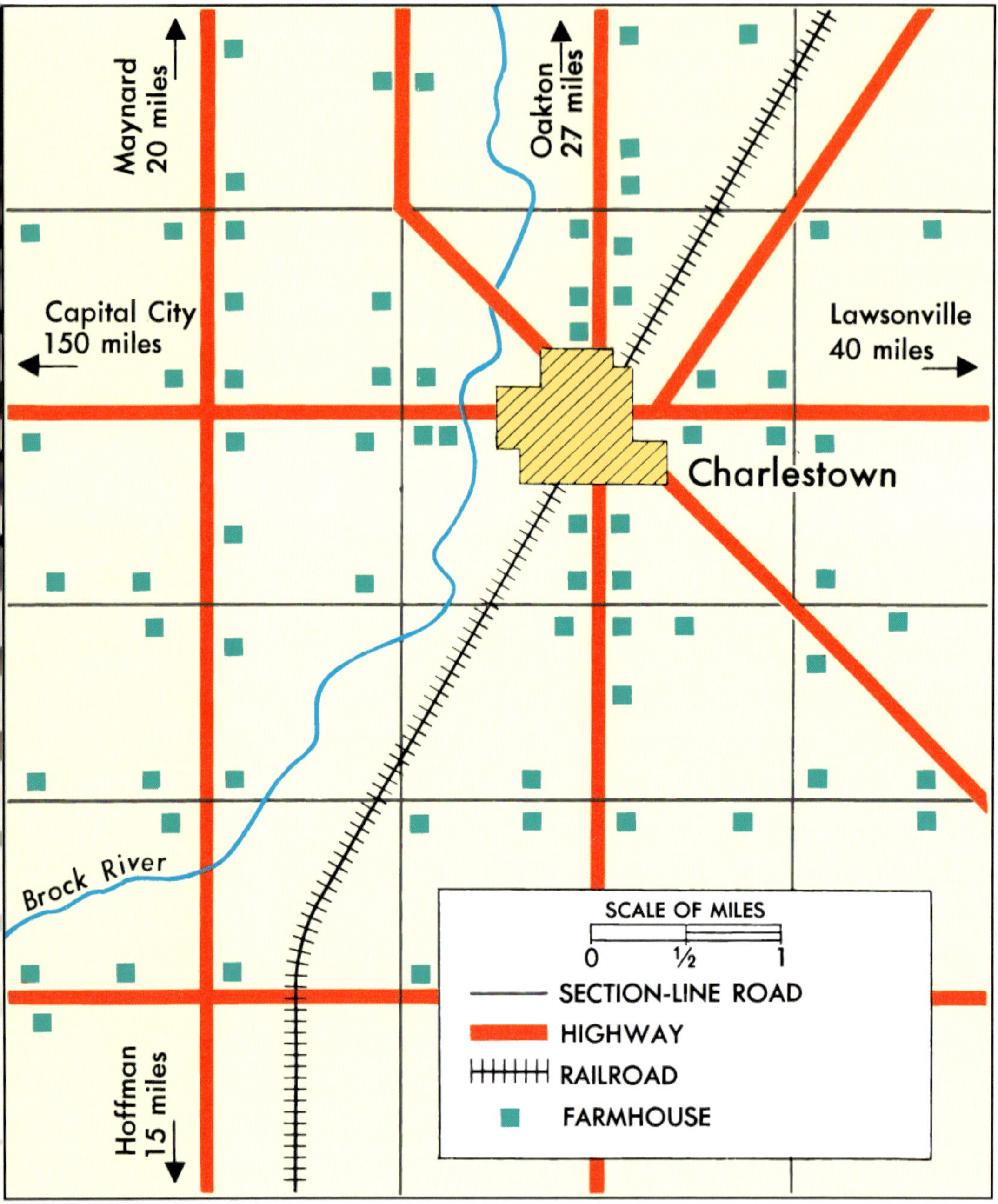

In an area that has been mapped for the distribution of public lands, older farmhouses stand on section-line roads. Newer homes are located on through highways and near the crossroads trading center.

parts of the world, farmers live on farmsteads located on the land they work. Their homes are said to be dispersed, or scattered. These dispersed settlements may be arranged in an orderly fashion, following a system of land survey, or they may be irregularly arranged over the land.

In other areas, farmers, fishers, miners, and lumberers live together in villages. Settlements of this nature are called agglomerated settlements. They are still rural, however. Their shapes vary from a line type of rural settlement to a compact circle or rectangle.

Other types of settlements have been developed by people engaged in manufacturing and trade. These are urban settlements, ranging in size from small villages to large metropolitan areas. An urban settlement is one where most people work to serve those outside the community. It has sections where shopping is done; areas where products are manufactured; and sections where people live, relax, and find entertainment.

The Association of Elements in an Area

Studying the location and arrangement of physical and human elements is only a part of the science of geography. Having established the patterns of different things, geography next calls for an explanation of these patterns. This is not based on causes and effects of the arrangement. Rather, it involves noting how two or more factors are associated in an area and whether a particular factor occurs in a given area only if another element is also present. These patterns are called areal associations.

An example of an areal association is the occurrence of productive farmlands in regions with a long growing season (that is, with abundant sunlight and warm temperatures over a long period), fertile soils, and relatively smooth landforms.

The relationship between climate and soil characteristics represents another areal association. These factors in turn help explain the differences in plant and animal life over Earth's surface. Temperature and rainfall are also related to natural plant and animal life.

A fundamental areal association is that of latitude and the amount of heat, or insolation, received from the sun. The amount of insolation received at any given place is explained by the angle of the sun's rays and the length of the day. For example, at a latitude of 40° N, June days are almost fifteen hours long, and the sun at noon is relatively high in the sky. The amount of heat received from sunlight is very high, and the days are warm. At the same latitude in December, the days are only about nine hours long, and the noon sun is low in the sky. Daily insolation is low and thus days are cold.

People and the Natural Environment

Geography also recognizes relationships that exist between people and the conditions of the natural environment. Climate, landforms, water supply, the presence or absence of minerals, and other natural characteristics of an area are related in many ways to the economic, social, and political affairs of people everywhere. For instance, the cold climate and short growing season of Norway help explain the kind of farming practiced. The presence of the sea and the rich fishing banks nearby are reasons why the Norwegians have become world famous for their fishing industry.

How people are related to the land depends upon their culture and its degree of industrial development as well as upon the nature of the

Codfish are being dried in the fishing village of Hamney in the Lofoten islands of Norway. Fishing has been the predominant industry since the islands' settlement in the twelfth century.

environment. Technical knowledge and skills enable people to use available resources to a fuller degree. This includes mining metals and coal to manufacture goods, and cultivating and fertilizing soil and irrigating land to improve the food supply.

Conservation and Conservationists

Conservation is the responsible stewardship of the environment to preserve natural ecosystems while ensuring that balanced consideration is also given to human needs for production and recreation. Most people believe that a major goal of conservation today is reasonable use of Earth's natural resources, which include water, soil, wildlife, forests, minerals, and fossil fuels.

Freshwater habitats must be kept clean for drinking and for recreational activities. Soils must be kept fertile, without the accumulation of toxic chemicals from pesticides or herbicides, to provide fruits and vegetables and to prevent poisoning of wildlife. Forests must be managed to provide not only lumber and pulpwood for paper products but also homes and food for native wildlife. The use of oil, coal, and minerals important for an industrial society must be carefully monitored to be certain that the supply does not dwindle too rapidly and that natural habitats are not degraded in the process of producing and using them.

Conservationists work to preserve the natural heritage for future generations. People concerned with conservation seek not only to maintain a high-quality environment suitable for both wildlife and humans but also to preserve the natural biological, genetic, and habitat diversity of ecosystems. This often involves preventing or minimizing environmental pollution from industrial, agricultural, urban, and domestic sources, including toxic chemicals, radioactive wastes, and elevated water temperatures. Conservationists also seek to prevent the waste of natural

(continued on the next page)

(continued from the previous page)

resources of any sort, to reduce consumption of energy and unnecessary commercial products, and to support recycling efforts.

Forests, grasslands, wildlife, and soil are examples of renewable natural resources. They can be regenerated through natural processes, and prudent management can maintain them at steady levels. The consumption of the limited supplies of nonrenewable fossil fuels such as coal, petroleum, and natural gas, whether wasteful or not, speeds their depletion. Conservation measures for fossil fuels involve reduced usage. Likewise, certain nonrenewable critical ores and metals, such as iron, aluminum (bauxite), and copper, have finite supplies. Controlled accessibility that sometimes calls for conservation measures, such as appropriate recycling programs, helps assure continued production.

Another goal of conservation is to preserve the natural beauty of a community. When land is mistreated, the countryside can become aesthetically unpleasant. Vacant lots covered with trash, bare roadsides, garbage-laden streams, and the unregulated sprawl of strip malls are ugly. Conservation also helps to preserve areas suitable for recreation. As cities grow crowded, natural areas are needed for people enjoying leisure time. People need city parks, wildlife preserves, and national parks; grass and trees bordering roads and highways; and clear streams.

Natural resources are a vital part of sustaining human life, and conservation measures are designed to control, manage, and preserve them so that they can be used and appreciated to the fullest. A proper conservation program incorporates effective measures so that all natural resources are managed in the best interest of everyone.

Geographers have long been concerned about the conservation of water, soil, minerals, and other natural resources. Many of these resources cannot be restored after they have been exhausted.

INTERACTIONS BETWEEN AREAS

Another focus of human geography pertains to the study of the interrelations of one area with another. It deals with the flow of goods, information, ideas, and people among areas. This area of focus is at the heart of the field called spatial interaction.

Studies in geography have covered the economic and political interactions between one part of the world and another. Until a few centuries ago areas of the world were almost cut off one from another due to limitations of transportation. Each area produced nearly everything it consumed. Improved means of transport since the Industrial Revolution have made possible the inexpensive, rapid, and large-scale exchange of goods. All parts of the world have now been brought into close economic relationships. Trade has been greatly accelerated and extended, and now is possible on a global scale.

In recent years, there have also been increasing interactions of a political nature among nations. In the twentieth century, there were two world wars and a number of lesser skirmishes among the major world powers. The search for security or the drive for expansion has given rise to a continual struggle for power. Several formulas for reducing conflicts have been advanced. These include alliances between individual countries and multination alliances such as the United Nations. Alliances commonly result in the flow of power—via people or weapons—from one country to another. Geography is concerned with the pattern of this flow.

Chapter 4

How Geography Is Studied

The distribution of things on the face of Earth can be investigated and analyzed in either of two ways. One approach is topical geography, or systematic geography. This approach involves investigation and analysis of the distribution of a single phenomenon throughout the world or within a specific area. Such a phenomenon might be Earth's landforms, its climate, its political divisions, or its agricultural characteristics.

The other approach is regional geography. It focuses attention upon a particular area or region. Within the region it investigates and analyzes the distribution and association of elements that give the region its distinctive character.

The science of geography is generally concerned with the distribution of phenomena at the present time. When the geography of some past time is analyzed—for example, the geography of New England in 1800—such studies are referred to as historical geographic studies. The art and science of recording the facts of geography in map form is the focus of the field of cartography.

TOPICAL GEOGRAPHY

Topical geography may be focused on physical or human phenomena. Analysis of the distribution of landforms, climates, water, soils, minerals, and similar factors falls within the realm of physical geography. Certain aspects

A map shows the elevation of the Appalachian Mountains. Topical geography may concern physical phenomena, such as the distribution of landforms or minerals, or human phenomena, such as mining operations.

of this branch, in turn, are sometimes studied separately. The specialty that treats the forms, size, and movements of Earth is called mathematical geography.

Topical geography may also be centered on the distribution of a human phenomenon. The analysis of the distribution of people's productive occupations, such as farming, mining, and manufacturing, comprises the field of economic geography. This field encompasses subspecialties such as the geography of agriculture, geography of manufacturing,

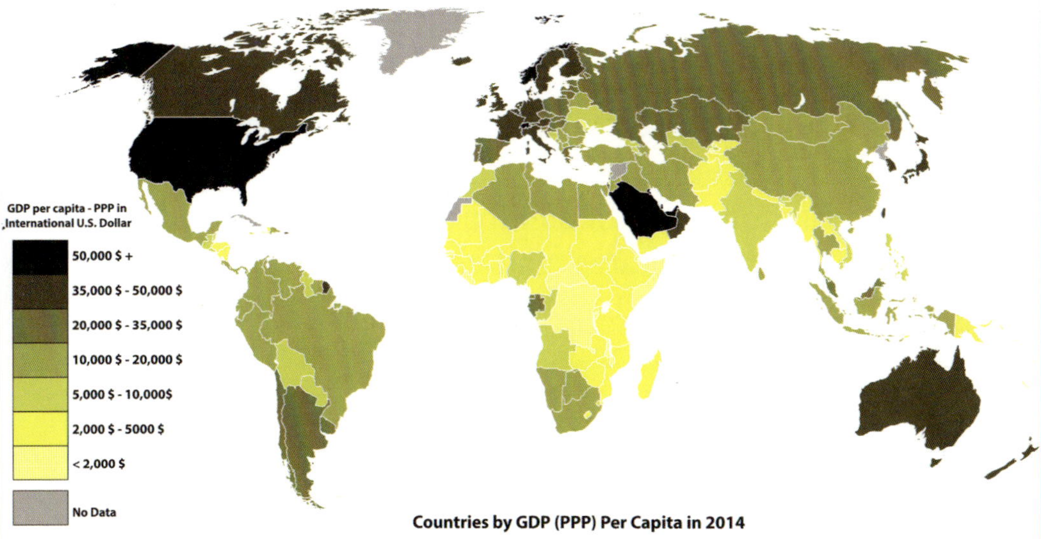

Economic geography deals with the relations of physical and economic conditions to the production and distribution of goods. This world map shows the gross domestic product (GDP) produced by a country, per capita, in 2014.

transportation geography, and commercial geography.

Political geography emphasizes the pattern of Earth's political sovereignties. Social geography includes the study of the dispersion of population and other factors, such as the distribution of the various religions. There are also a geography of education and a geography of the arts.

A specialized field of topical geography, known as urban geography, is devoted to analyzing the distribution of cities and of things within cities.

REGIONAL GEOGRAPHY

In regional geography, analysis is concentrated on associations that give character to a particular area. The area may be continental in size, or it may be subdivided into units such as countries, states, and counties. Subdivisions of the world based on similarities of human life form cultural regions. Subdivisions based on similarities of natural conditions form physical regions. Thus, there is a geography of North America, a geography of the United States, a geography of New England, and a geography of Boston.

Historical Geography

Historical geography is the geographic study of a place or region at a specific time or period in the past, or the study of geographic change in a place or region over a period of time. The writings of Herodotus in the fifth century BCE, particularly his discussion of how the Nile River delta formed, probably provide the earliest example of what would be called historical geography today. Historical

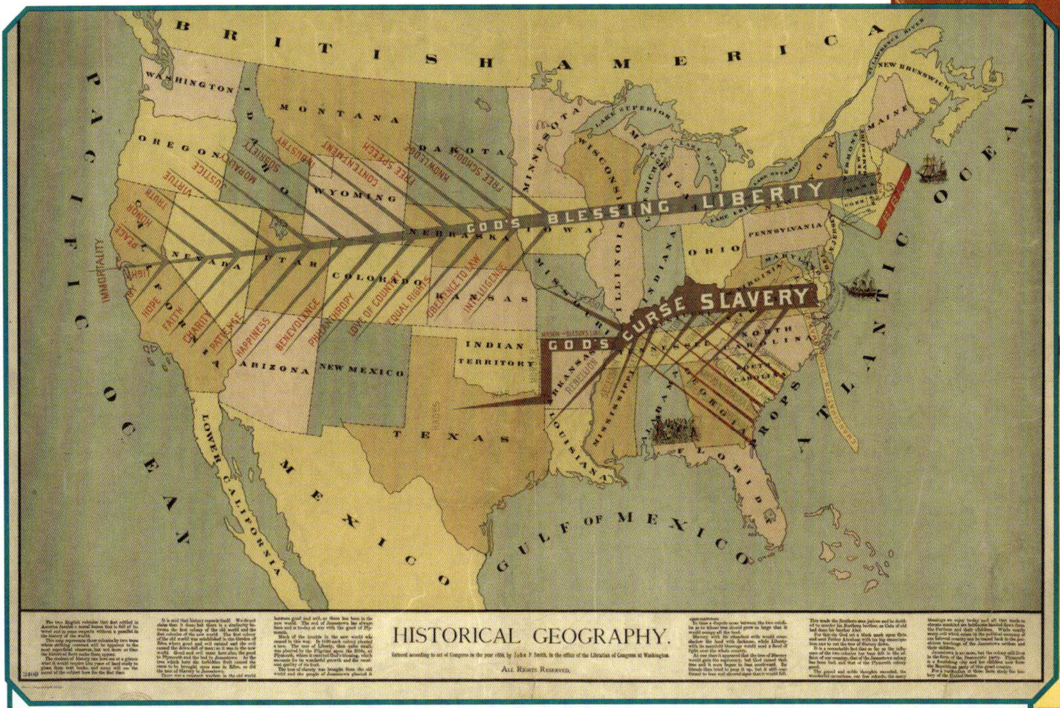

Stylized trees were placed on a US map in 1888 to depict the North's victory of liberty over the South's slavery from the colonial period through the Civil War. Historical geography studies historical events in a place at a specific time in the past.

geography, as the study of past geographies, remained a relatively undeveloped field of study until the seventeenth century, when Philipp Clüver, considered the founder of historical geography, published a historical geography of Germany, combining knowledge of the classics with knowledge of the land.

In the nineteenth century, the importance of geography as the basis for understanding history was taught in many universities, particularly in Great Britain. Geography as the basis for understanding history changed to the geographic influence upon historical events in the early twentieth century. The work of Ellen Churchill Semple used this environmental deterministic interpretation of history. From the 1930s, historical geography gained prominence through studies of sequent occupance (human occupation of a specific region over intervals of historic time) initiated by Derwent S. Whittlesey and Carl O. Sauer. The establishment of the *Journal of Historical Geography* (1975) and historical-geography research groups by the Institute of British Geographers (1973) and the Association of American Geographers (1979) served to vindicate the historical approach in geography.

Cartography

Cartography, the study of maps and the art and science of making them, is a subdiscipline of geography, but many other disciplines, especially in the social sciences, also have mapmakers. In addition to recording geographic information, mapping may involve the superimposition of political, cultural, or other nongeographical divisions onto the representation of a geographical area.

Cartography is an ancient discipline that dates from the prehistoric depiction of hunting and fishing territories. The Babylonians mapped the world in a flattened, disk-shaped form, but Claudius Ptolemaeus (Ptolemy) established the basis for subsequent efforts in the second century CE with his eight-volume work *Geōgraphikē hyphēgēsis* (*Guide to Geography*), which showed a spherical Earth. Maps produced during the Middle Ages followed Ptolemy's guide, but they used Jerusalem as the central feature and placed East at the top. Those representations are often called T-maps because they show only three continents (Europe, Asia, and Africa), separated by the "T" formed by the Mediterranean Sea

Ptolemy's map of the world, shown in a fifteenth-century copy, includes only Europe, Asia, and northern Africa. The Americas, southern Africa, Australia, the Pacific islands, and Antarctica were unknown to Ptolemy in the second century CE.

and the Nile River. More accurate geographical representation began in the fourteenth century when portolan (seamen's) charts were compiled for navigation.

The discovery of the New World by Europeans led to the need for new techniques in cartography, particularly for the systematic representation on a flat surface of the features of a curved surface. This is called a projection; familiar examples include the Mercator projection, cylindrical projections, and Lambert conformal projections. During

GEOGRAPHIC INFORMATION SYSTEMS (GIS)

A geographic information system, or GIS, is a computer system for analyzing geographical data. It is capable of capturing, storing, manipulating, analyzing, and displaying data in two- or three-dimensional maps. The system's ability to combine different kinds of data into a single map allows the user to see relationships between the data that might not otherwise be clear. GIS has a great number of applications in a wide range of areas, such as the planning of public facilities and services.

The first step in using GIS is inputting data relevant to the question at hand. The data must be linked to specific geographic places; for example, they may be tagged to an address or to a grid based on coordinates of latitude and longitude. A GIS can use data that come from a number of sources, such as databases, satellite images, aerial photographs, or paper maps that are scanned into the system. When necessary—as in the case of paper maps—the system converts the geographical data into a computer-usable form. This process is known as digitizing. Then the system combines the different pieces of data to produce a new map. Because the data are organized and stored in "layers" that can be added or removed from the new map, the user can combine the information in different ways to study relationships and patterns.

GIS has become an important tool for environmental and urban planners, retail site analysts, water resource specialists, and other professionals whose work relies on maps. One example of GIS's many applications is the analysis of crimes by police. Police departments keep databases in which they record crimes by type and by the location and time they were

(continued on page 65)

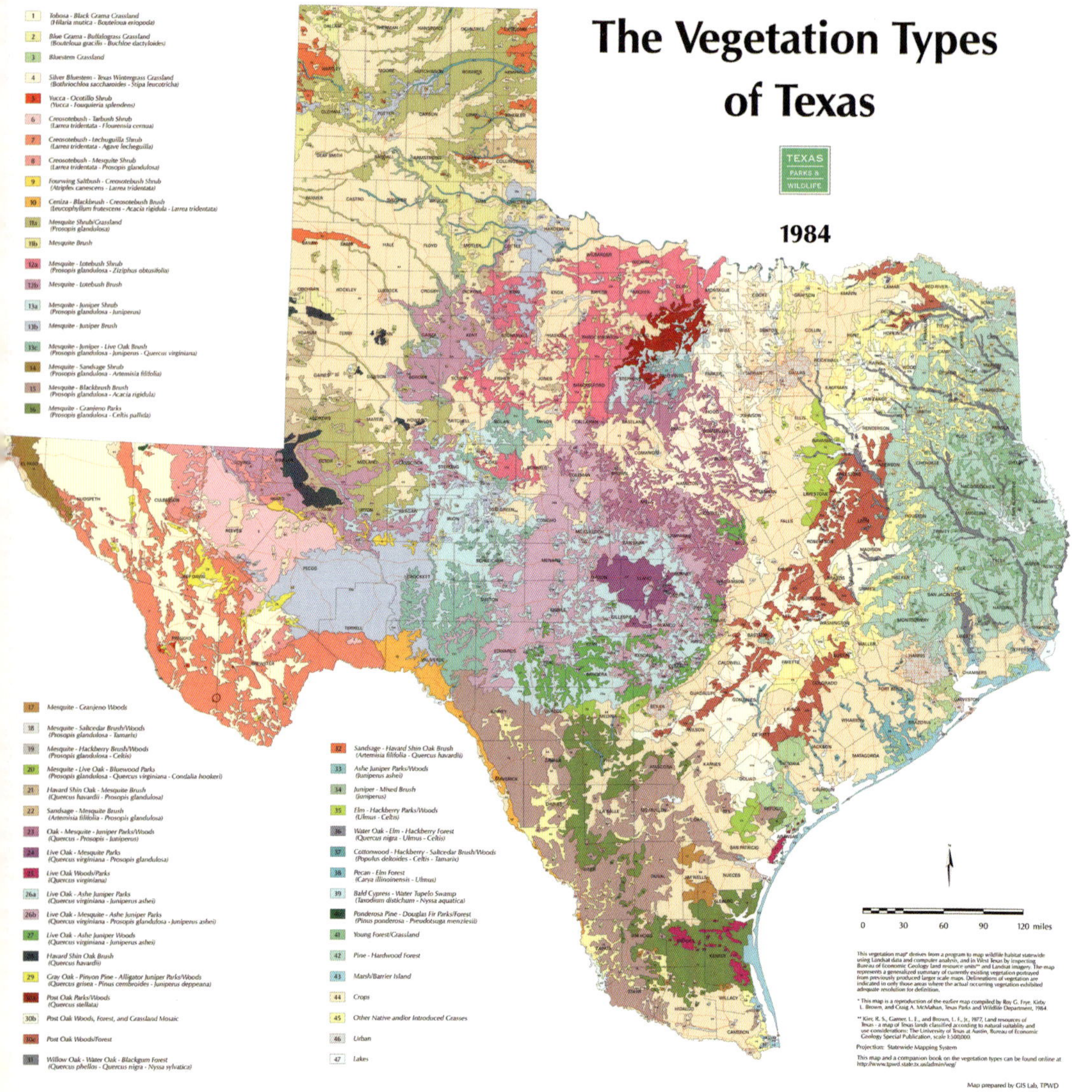

The Texas Parks and Wildlife Department's GIS Lab created a map that depicts the types of vegetation in Texas. Datasets for GIS maps often can be downloaded from websites that use geographic information in planning and research.

(continued from page 63)

committed. A GIS uses the location information to plot each crime on a digital map. One layer of the map might show burglaries, while other layers show robberies, motor vehicle thefts, and other crimes. Additional map layers can show information such as streets, public transportation, businesses, and schools. By examining the different layers of such a map, the police can find crime hot spots and patterns—for example, a series of robberies clustered near train stations in a city neighborhood during the evening rush hour. Police can use this information to shape their response to the crimes. They might send additional officers to patrol near train stations at that time of day, ask employees at the train stations to be on alert for suspicious activity, and warn commuters to be especially watchful in the area.

the seventeenth and eighteenth centuries, there was a vast outpouring of printed maps of ever-increasing accuracy and sophistication. Systematic surveys were undertaken involving triangulation that greatly improved map reliability and precision. Noteworthy among the scientific methods introduced later was the use of the telescope for determining the length of a degree of longitude.

Modern cartography largely involves the use of aerial and, increasingly, satellite photographs as a base for any desired map or chart. The procedures for translating photographic data into maps are governed by the principles of photogrammetry and yield a degree of accuracy previously unattainable. The remarkable improvements in satellite photography since the late twentieth century and the general availability on the internet of satellite images have made possible the creation of Google Earth and other databases that are widely available online. Satellite photography has also been used to create highly detailed maps of features of the moon and of several planets in our solar system and their satellites. In addition, the use of geographic information systems (GIS) has been indispensible in expanding the scope of cartographic subjects.

Chapter 5

Maps and Globes

The arrangement of things over Earth and the interactions between two or more areas can be presented with clarity and simplicity on maps. A map is a graphical representation, usually in two dimensions, of an area, such as Earth's surface, an ocean floor, the night sky, or a neighborhood. Although maps are used in many other studies, in geography they are a constantly essential tool.

Because world maps are drawn on a flat surface, they cannot show Earth's curved surface without significant distortions. Globes help to counter that problem. A globe is a spherical representation of a planet's surface or another large area. It is usually mounted on an axle that allows for rotation. A globe can show a planet without distortion because of its rounded shape, although Earth—as well as most other planets—is not a perfect sphere but bulges a bit at the equator. People use

A globe presents the physical features of Earth close to their true shapes. A globe is mounted on an axle that permits rotation.

globes less often than maps because of their bulk and greater cost.

In geography, maps and globes are useful for studying both the physical Earth and the movements of people, goods, and information. Maps can be misleading, however; their crisp lines, bright colors, and labels may not always accurately represent areas of interest. All maps and globes have some distortions, deletions, and simplifications associated with the intended use of the map, the makers' biases, political influences, and other factors.

The words "map," "chart," and "plat" are used somewhat interchangeably. The connotations of use, however, are distinctive: charts for navigation purposes (nautical and aeronautical), plats (in a property-boundary sense) for land-line references and ownership, and maps for general reference.

MAP PROJECTIONS: NECESSARY DISTORTIONS

All maps make selective omissions and distortions, beginning when an image is transferred from a globe. If Earth were flat, it could easily be displayed; however, its spherical shape cannot be flattened without distorting distances (areas), shapes, or directions. Experts now use mathematical formulas to help make maps; such renderings are called map projections because they were originally made by shining a lamp inside a transparent globe to trace projected images on a screen. The image shifted according to the placement of the lamp and screen. Every projection has pros and cons and may be disputed for political, academic, and aesthetic motives. Although an infinite variety of projections can be created, the more popular are cylindrical, conic, planar, equal-area, and so-called compromise projections.

(continued on the next page)

Gerardus Mercator's son, Rumold, created this twin-hemispherical world map, "A Comprehensive Description of the World," in 1587. It was based on the elder Mercator's projection technique that was first used on a map of the world in 1569.

(*continued from the previous page*)

Cylindrical projections are among the most commonly used, partly because navigators prefer their straight north-south lines (meridians of longitude). To make this projection, a cylinder is placed over the globe. Its sides touch only along the equator, the only latitude where sizes are shown accurately. After the source of light is applied and the lines from the globe are transferred to the cylinder, the cylinder is cut and rolled out flat.

The most famous cylindrical projection, the Mercator—devised by Flemish cartographer Gerardus Mercator in the sixteenth century—remains highly controversial. In the 1800s, its popularity was unequaled. Some users liked how it made British (and other European) lands appear larger than they were. It remained popular during the Cold War, when its exaggeration of the size of the Soviet Union highlighted fears of Communist aggression. Among other distortions, it makes Greenland seem larger than South America, although the island is only one-eighth the size of the continent. The Mercator projection is still used, though many individuals prefer other, more accurate, projections.

READING A MAP OR GLOBE

Map styles and symbols vary across cultures, but most published maps share certain

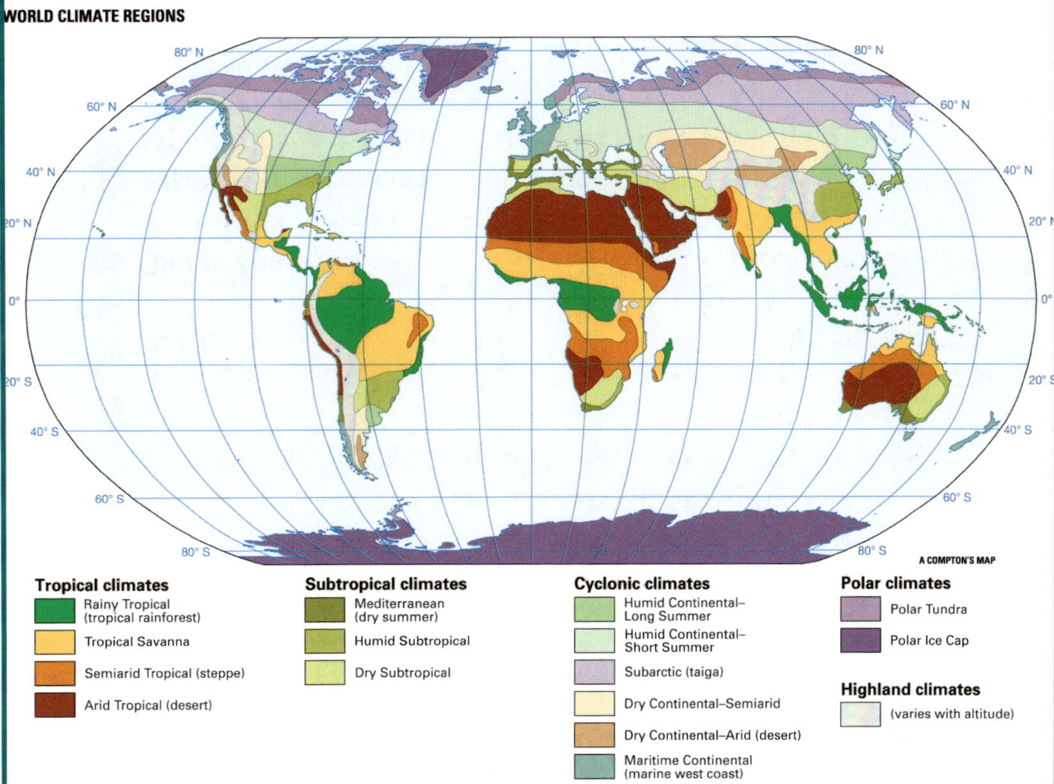

This map of world climates shows approximations. For example, an area marked as an arid tropical desert might actually share characteristics with a semiarid tropical steppe. The map includes a grid of latitude and longitude and a color key.

details in common. Maps should show a date of compilation or publication to give the user a frame of reference. They may include place names (labels), a scale (to compare sizes), a grid (to find locations), a guide to symbols, and an arrow pointing north or a compass rose showing the four cardinal directions.

Intuitive Searches and Basic Grids

One strategy for reading a map is to look first for familiar shapes or outlines (the Florida peninsula, the Horn of Africa, the boot of Italy), oceans and inlets (the long Red Sea or the shorter Persian Gulf), the telltale arcs of mountains (the Andes as the spine of South America; the Himalayas north of India, covering Nepal and Bhutan), or the blue swoops of rivers and fanning deltas. It may be helpful to find a familiar city, road, or other landmark. After obtaining a general overview of the map, more complex symbols and information can be explored.

To locate the city of Adams, Massachusetts, on this map with an alphanumeric grid, you would first look it up in the map index. Opposite the city's name would be the symbol B2, signifying that Adams is located on the map where the row down from B overlaps the row right from 2.

Basic map grids place letters across the top (A, B, C, etc.) and numbers on the side (1, 2, 3, etc.), or vice versa. If a map index lists a site as B4, for example, a person can trace down from the B and across from the 4 to find the sought-after destination. Most tourist maps and road maps use this kind of basic grid.

Latitude and Longitude

World maps show lines of latitude and longitude, a coordinate system by means of which the position or location of any place on Earth's surface can be determined and described. Lines of longitude, or meridians, are drawn from the North Pole to the South Pole and show distances east or west from the prime meridian (0 degrees longitude), running through Greenwich, England. Greenwich was chosen for the prime meridian because when the system of latitude and longitude was established, Great Britain was a world leader in exploration and map making. Greenwich was the home of Britain's royal observatory.

Lines of latitude, which intersect meridians at right angles, are called parallels because they parallel the equator (0 degrees latitude), from which they measure north or south. Both lines of latitude and longitude are measured in degrees, minutes, and seconds.

There are 360 degrees in a circle, and longitude measures to 180 degrees east or west (180 + 180 = 360) until arriving at a point in the mid-Pacific Ocean, on or near the International Date Line (the imaginary line running between the North Pole and the South Pole and distinguishing each calendar day from the next). Likewise, latitude runs to the North Pole (90 degrees north) and the South Pole (90 degrees south)—adding up to 360 degrees if we see a globe in cross section (90 + 90 on one side, 90 + 90 on the other). Each degree is divided into 60 minutes, each minute 60 seconds. Computers can show these as decimals: for example, 21 degrees and 45 minutes is 21.75 degrees, because 45 minutes is three-fourths of a degree, or 0.75 as a decimal.

The combination of meridians of longitude and parallels of latitude establishes a framework or grid by means of which exact positions can be determined in reference to the prime meridian and the equator. Thus a point described as 40 degrees north, 30 degrees west (the two numbers together are called coordinates) is located 40 degrees of arc north of the equator and 30 degrees of arc west of the Greenwich meridian.

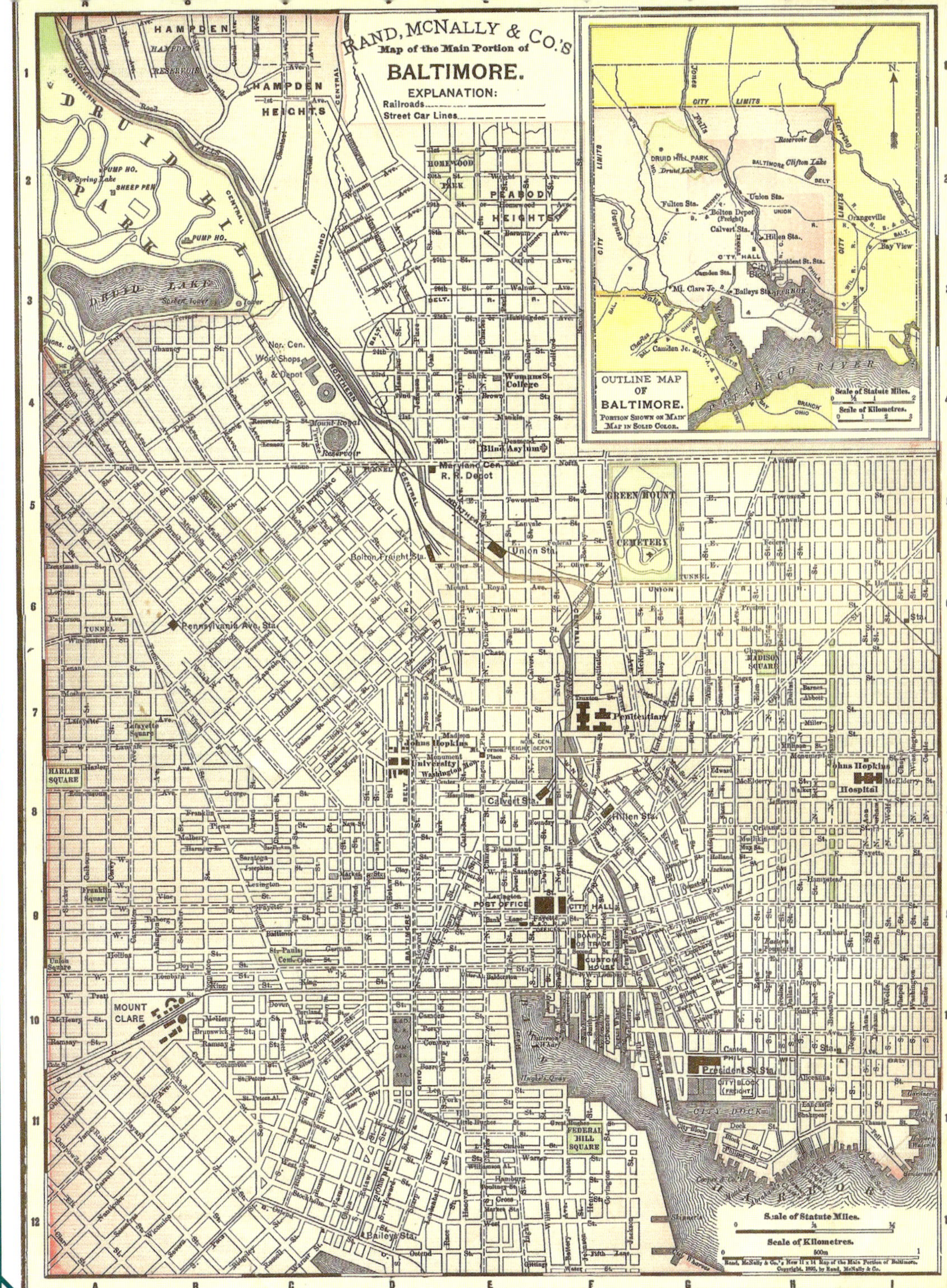

A map of Baltimore, Maryland, created in 1891, has an alphanumeric grid and a scale (*bottom right and in the inset*). The scale refers to the size of the representation on the map as compared to the size of the object on the ground.

SCALE

A scale is a mathematical relationship, or ratio, between actual sizes and the sizes shown on a map. If one centimeter on the map equals 10 actual kilometers, the ratio can be written 1:1,000,000 (there are 1 million centimeters in 10 kilometers) or it may be shown as a line marked with distances. There is no ideal map scale. It is a compromise between two conflicting aims—the desire to show details while covering as much area as possible. Large-scale maps cover smaller areas (just as cameras with large zoom lenses provide close-ups), whereas small-scale maps show wider areas with less detail.

MAP SYMBOLS

Some map symbols are readily understood, but others require a legend (also called a key or index of symbols) because they vary by culture, mapping custom, and individual choice. For example, Native Americans at one time used cross-shapes to indicate stars, whereas Spanish conquistadors used them to indicate churches and towns. Blue lines were used in mid-twentieth-century American road maps for back roads, made famous in travel writer William Least Heat-Moon's book *Blue Highways: A Journey into America* (1982).

On conventional maps, black lines usually symbolize roads, tick-marked lines are railroads, circles or stars are cities, and shading or dark lines are contours (lines that indicate elevations). Green and brown may shade real-world features (green forests, brown deserts), but colors sometimes indicate elevations. This coloring may cause confusion where, for example, green shading (indicating low elevation) covers a hot, dry, brown desert.

Map and Globe Orientation

People often assume that the top of a map should point north; however, map orientation is a choice, not a natural law, and it is subject to political, economic, religious, and aesthetic desires. Muslim mapmakers such as twelfth-century geographer ash-Sharif al-Idrisi often placed south at the top of their works. Many medieval European maps were oriented toward the east, out of the belief that the Holy Land and the biblical Garden of Eden were the most important areas in the world. The word "orient" (as in "map orientation") derives from the Latin *oriens* ("east"), so to orient oneself once meant to face east or to place east at the top.

Nothing is inherently wrong with a map topped by the South Pole or Chile, yet it seems odd to many people. To some, north-oriented maps reinforce notions of European and North American power, of being on top of the world. Video games and GPS (global positioning systems) in phones or in cars allow the user to change map orientations and to view landscapes at oblique angles. "You Are Here" maps (in shopping malls, at tourist sites, at festivals, etc.) are most useful when oriented by line-of-sight, rather than by compass points.

ADVANTAGES OF GLOBES AND ATLASES

Although globes are unwieldy and more expensive than maps, they show how Earth is tilted (about 23.5 degrees) and how this relates to day lengths and the seasons. For example, when in a dark room, a person can shine a flashlight (representing the sun) on one side of a globe to demonstrate how sunlight reaches half the tilted Earth while leaving the rest in shadow, according to the season. Globes also show shapes, sizes, and lines without distortions.

Globes can help people plan long-distance travel routes. If a person pulls a string between two cities on its curved surface, the string will follow the shortest path, called a great circle route. On such a route, airplanes from the United States to Europe fly north-northeast rather than straight east, though on a map it is easy to plot—mistakenly—the eastern route.

Globes often display an analemma, a figure-eight-shaped diagram showing the subsolar point (the latitude where the sun reaches its highest, 90-degree angle in the sky and is directly overhead) on each date of the year. Other globes indicate the subsolar point by marking dates on a line that undulates from tropic to tropic and crosses the equator.

Computer maps and computerized atlases offer multimedia games, quick searches, and simulated 3D globes and maps, but print atlases remain popular. Both print and electronic atlases are created by teams of skilled writers, editors, cartographers, and artists. With a medley of reference data, indexes, maps, photos, and diagrams, they offer enough variety for repeat reading and browsing.

TYPES OF MAPS

Maps can be classified in different ways; three of the most basic map categories are reference maps, illustrative maps, and analytic maps. Reference maps can be used like an encyclopedia to provide important information about an area, such as the location of streets or landforms. Illustrative maps show the distribution of specific phenomena or the spatial correlation of two or more phenomena on Earth's surface. Analytical maps suggest ideas that can be tested by mathematical and statistical techniques. The latter type of map is used mostly by professional geographers in their research. The reference and illustrative maps are used in everyday affairs.

An example of a reference map is a road map. Drivers refer to such maps to find out how to get from one place to another. The weather map reproduced in daily newspapers is an example of an illustrative map. It shows how temperatures, precipitation, winds, and pressure are related in space. Illustrative maps also may show connections among various parts of Earth. Trade maps are illustrative maps.

The most popular maps are road maps, political maps (showing countries, states, or counties), physical maps (of mountains, rivers, etc.), and thematic maps (focusing on one or two themes, such as income, livestock, or health insurance). General reference maps include a mixture of information, as do many road, political, and physical maps.

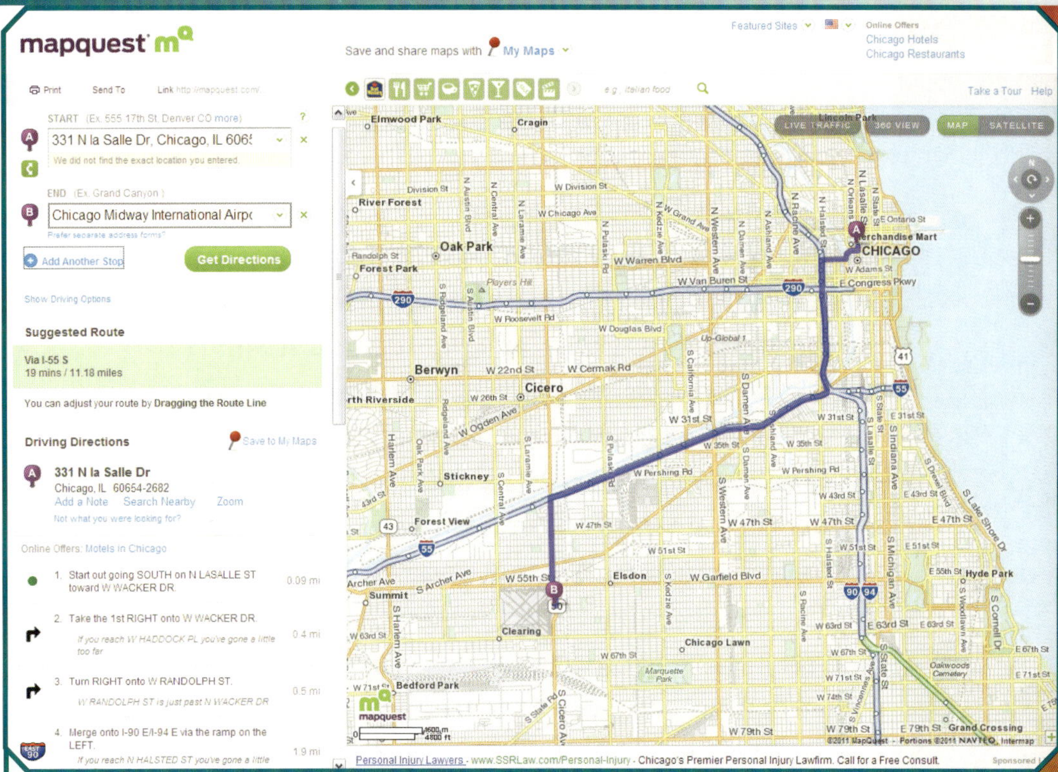

A MapQuest.com screenshot shows Chicago, Illinois, and the surrounding area. GPS and web-based map services can access maps of any place in the world and obtain driving directions by providing starting and ending locations.

Transportation Maps

Road maps and street maps blend political and physical data. GPS and web-based aids such as Google Maps and MapQuest include them as base maps. When these are outdated, however, mistakes can occur, such as green fields appearing where malls have been built. As a GPS is moved, it plots satellite coordinates on the base map, and the display shows a shifting, turning icon to give the illusion that the map is being generated on the run.

Some maps are designed for cyclists, tourists, or hikers. Aviation charts mark air routes and major obstacles or features on the ground. Shipping charts do the same for maritime traffic. Since at least the early 1900s, commuters have used transit maps on metropolitan buses, trains, and subways. Simplified transit maps, called diagrammatic maps, were introduced in 1933 in London, England. Seldom more than lists of stations along a line, these omit or abbreviate street names, directions, and landmarks useful for orientation. Although diagrammatic maps can be useful, their lack of detail may be confusing to millions of passengers each year.

POLITICAL MAPS

Countries, provinces, and counties are the focus of political maps. Their bright colors and crisp borderlines encourage geographic literacy but are deceptively simple: they tell only partial truths about nations and borders that are shifting or arbitrary. These maps do not show, for example, that many borders are not even lined by walls or fences. Moreover, they eventually change as countries disintegrate (such as the former Soviet Union and

Yugoslavia), are renamed (Zaire/Congo and Myanmar/Burma), or reunify (Germany).

Physical Maps

Rivers, lakes, mountains, hills, deserts, vegetation, and other natural features are on physical maps. Beyond Earth's surface, these maps may detail seafloors, ocean and air currents, and subterranean resources. Topographic maps symbolize relief with dark shading or hachure and rill marks (short lines indicating slope). Some show elevations with contours (lines of progressively greater height). Contours drawn close together indicate steeper slopes (grades, or gradients).

Older maps depict highlands with idealized sketches of molehills or snowcapped peaks rather than with detailed sketches of mountains and plateaus. Some maps and globes are made with raised bumps along mountain ranges. An entertaining and useful memory tool, this kind of vertical exaggeration nevertheless gives a misleading sense of elevation, since Earth's diameter is nearly 8,000 miles (12,875 kilometers) while mountains rise less than 5.5 miles (9 kilometers).

Thematic Maps

A map that focuses on the symbolic display of statistics, or themes, is called a thematic map.

These maps may focus on language, religion, income, population density, or any other kind of measurable data. Some depict processes such as toxic spills, seismicity, or the geologic history of continental drift. The most common types use shading, line patterns, or dots to indicate different measures. Flow maps often use arrows to indicate change or movement. Choropleth maps use shades of color to represent different measures or values. For example, US states with higher population density might be shaded a darker brown than those states with a relatively sparse population.

Thematic maps can be misleading because they eliminate marginal statistics and minority views. An election (suffrage) map, for instance, might shade a state red if 50.1 percent of its voters opt for a Republican candidate; however, overgeneralizing by calling this a "red state" (as news media often do) unfairly ignores the other 49.9 percent of the electorate there.

Cartograms

Another statistical mapping device is the cartogram, which is sometimes called a specialized thematic map. Cartograms involve more artwork than normal maps, as they freely distort shapes, directions, and areas beyond normal ranges to illustrate or explain statistics. A cartogram "weights" the sizes of states, provinces, or countries to reflect values: a large number swells an area while a small number shrinks it. For example, a comparison of weapons exports by country would show a bloated United States (the world's top arms exporter) as would cartograms of prison populations, internet users, or miles driven. A population cartogram would bloat the outlines of India and China.

Mapmaking

Maps have been created for thousands of years with different intentions, materials, and results. There is no single history of mapmaking, but even the earliest maps were linked with religious and social (political) power. Increasingly, maps have been used to claim lands, mark borders, plan military actions, and assist in mining, farming, and exploration.

Mapmaking requires knowledge about the world and techniques for gathering, analyzing, and displaying information. Access to these processes has accelerated with more rapid ships, trains, and automobiles. In the early twentieth century, zeppelins and airplanes boosted the accuracy of maps with the previously unexpected details of aerial photography.

In the 1960s, as computing was in its infancy, mapmakers began to develop databases and mapping software. Initially, programming was slow and cumbersome, requiring large stacks of punch cards, and that era's room-sized computers were even more unwieldy. Supercomputers and mainframe systems became faster and a bit smaller in the 1970s.

The widespread availability of personal computers accelerated map work in the late twentieth century. However, few computers produced large, high-resolution images cheaply or easily, so maps continued to be handmade and then reprinted or photocopied for most publications, including atlases and encyclopedias. Even the maps featured in video games left much to be desired. Most were heavily pixilated; some were simple outlines (aids for in-game navigation) only, although some turn-based military strategy games were built around increasingly interactive maps. In the 1990s, advances in graphics, memory, and computing speeds brought fictitious maps to the forefront, particularly in fantasy and strategy games.

The 1990s also saw rapid advances in computer programming and the distribution of maps on CDs and, increasingly, the internet. Data from previously independent sources (such as air-quality surveys, traffic data, and residential maps) were compiled into GIS, which allowed geographers to discover new connections while creating dynamic, innovative maps.

Web-based mapping developed rapidly from its 1990s origins, when even publishers and government agencies had struggled to produce attractive, useful maps that could be downloaded or viewed without major delays. Multimedia, including video and animations, became common features on web-based maps, as applications for the compiling, analysis, and publishing of maps spread. Although people would always find reasons to sketch quick maps for driving or hiking directions, the dominion of handmade maps was ending.

In the early twenty-first century, web-based maps matched—and often surpassed—the CDs and DVDs from a few years previous. Interactive maps became vital parts of educational, commercial, and nonprofit websites, censuses, and other official reports. Maps for entertainment in video games often led the way in terms of interactivity and complexity. Meanwhile, high-resolution satellite images became available and affordable.

Internet mashups (maps of mixed data formats, projections, and styles) provided by Google Maps and MapQuest used these technological advances to offer options for showing either a road map, a satellite view, or a combined view. Mashup satellite views can be helpful, but sometimes their high level of detail is confusing. To market these as interactive road, tourist, and consumer maps, mashups must work to update their base maps frequently with cars specifically outfitted to carry digital cameras and GPS units.

CHAPTER 6

THE HISTORY OF GEOGRAPHY

The earliest geographers were actually surveyors and mapmakers, but in ancient Greece, where geography as a discipline really began to emerge, they were natural philosophers with a broad range of knowledge and talents. The best known of the ancient scholars was Strabo (64BCE?–23CE?), a Greek historian and geographer. His *Geography* is the only existing work covering the peoples and countries known to the Greeks and Romans.

THE AGE OF DISCOVERY

During the Age of Discovery, beginning in the fifteenth century, geography experienced a new birth after centuries of neglect. Geographers provided the impetus for many expeditions and vastly increased the world's knowledge about itself. The rediscovery of an important ancient Greek work—Ptolemy's *Guide to Geography*—greatly increased interest in cartography. Developments in printing and engraving helped make maps more widely available. Geographers were also able to make maps increasingly accurate, partly because better instruments were being used for astronomical observation and navigation of ships.

The magnetic compass had reached Europe by the twelfth century. Within a hundred years or so, sea captains learned to rely on it for direction-finding. In addition, navigators began using devices known as the cross-staff and the astrolabe to determine a ship's latitude (north-south position). Little by little it became safer for sailors to venture into unknown seas. Sailors made discoveries that allowed cartographers to make better maps that showed more of the world; these maps in turn inspired and aided further voyages of exploration.

NATIONAL SURVEY ORGANIZATIONS

By the eighteenth century, governments and learned societies had taken over the sponsorship of exploration and had replaced

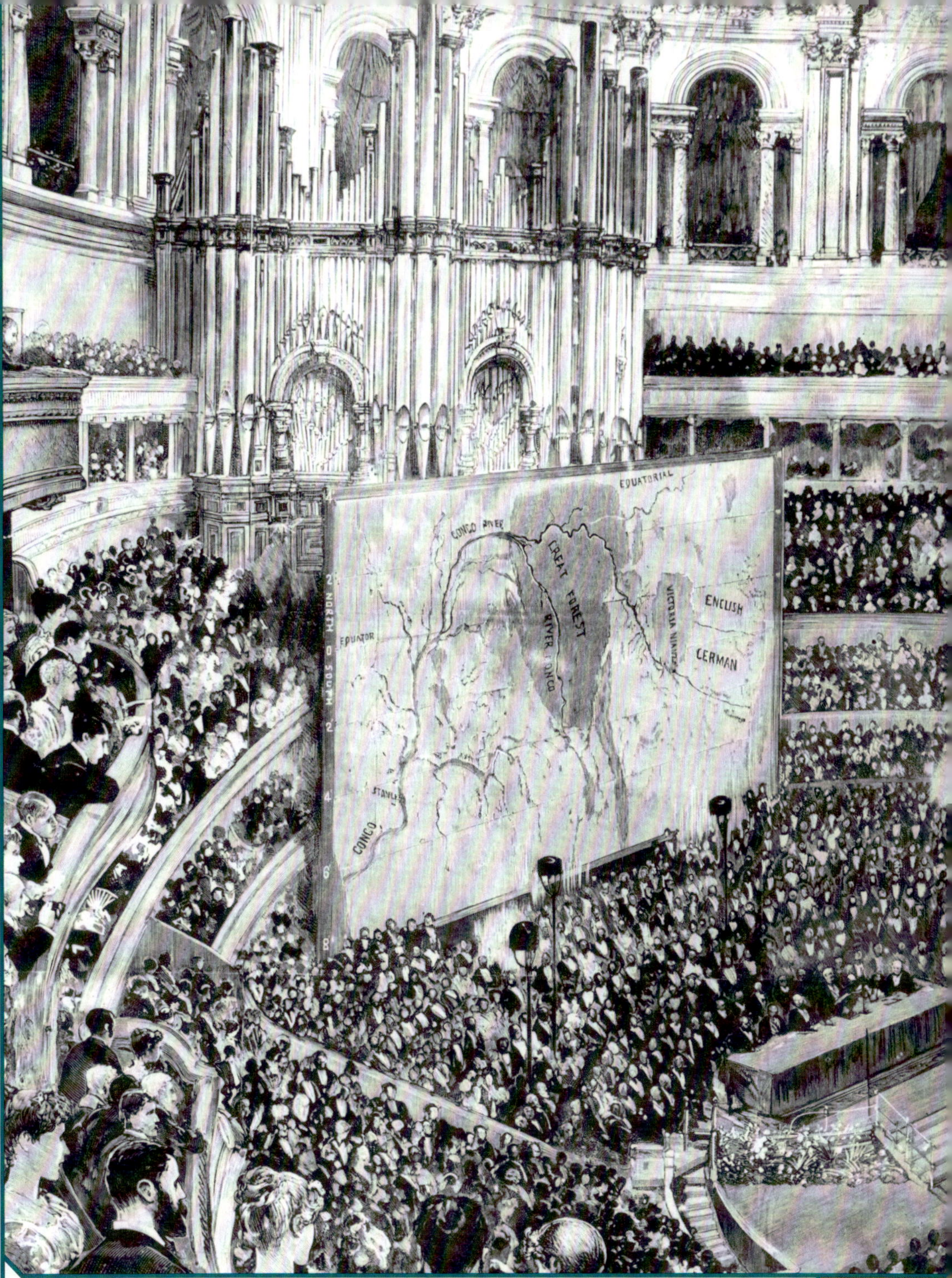

Sir Henry Stanley, who explored Central Africa, lectures before the Royal Geographical Society in London in 1890. Organizations such as this supported surveying and mapping trips to foster geographic knowledge.

geographers with professional surveyors and mapmakers—as in the earliest times. There was an outburst of topographic activity in the eighteenth century, reinforced to some extent by increasing civil needs for basic data. Many countries of Europe began to undertake the systematic topographic mapping of their territories. Such surveys required facilities and capabilities far beyond the means of private cartographers who had theretofore provided for most map needs. Originally exclusively military, national survey organizations gradually became civilian in character. The Ordnance Survey of Britain, the Institut Géographique National of France, and the Landestopographie of Switzerland are examples.

In other countries, such as the United States, where defense considerations were not paramount, civilian organizations—such as the US Geological Survey and the National Ocean Service (originally Survey)—were assigned responsibility for domestic mapping tasks. Only when World War II brought requirements for the mapping of many foreign areas did the US military become involved on a large scale, with the expansion of the Oceanographic Office (Navy), Aeronautical Chart Service (Air Force), and the US Army Topographic command.

Elaborate national surveys were undertaken only in certain countries. The rest of the world remained largely unmapped until World War II. The war brought great progress in mapping, particularly of the unmapped parts of Earth; an appraisal by the US Air Force indicated that in 1940 less than 10 percent of the world was mapped in sufficient detail for even the meager requirements of pilot charts. A major program of aerial photography and reconnaissance mapping was developed. Vast areas of the unmapped parts of the world were covered during the war years, and the resulting World Aeronautical Charts have provided generalized information for other purposes since that time. Many countries have used the basic data to publish temporary map coverage until their more detailed surveys can be completed.

GEOGRAPHY AS A DISCIPLINE

In the 1800s, two Germans—Alexander von Humboldt and Carl Ritter—were the first to write and teach as academic geographers. Since their day most geographers have been scholars, scientists, and teachers. Geography, through the efforts of such organizations as the Royal

Artist Joseph Stieler painted the German naturalist and geographer Alexander von Humboldt in 1843. Humboldt was a pioneer in studying the relationship between a region's geography and its flora and fauna.

Geographical and American Geographical Societies, has become firmly established as an academic discipline. The knowledge, techniques, and skills of trained geographers have also made their services valuable to many outside the academic world. Many governmental and business agencies employ geographers as planners, researchers, consultants, and scientists.

Since the latter part of the twentieth century, geography has been characterized by several trends. One such trend is specialization. Geography has always combined the work of many disciplines, but today's geographer is more likely to be an expert in only one aspect than in the subject as a whole. Thus there are agricultural geographers, climatologists, arid-zone specialists, and so on.

Geography in the modern day has become highly quantified—that is, it depends on mathematical models and statistical analyses. This trend has been advanced and encouraged by expanding computer technology. However, criticism of quantification's reliance on numbers and formulas has led to a trend toward a more humanistic geography that attempts to understand human emotions and reactions as they affect matters of space and location. In the United States in particular, an additional trend has led

ALEXANDER VON HUMBOLDT

Along with Napoleon, Alexander von Humboldt (1769–1859) was one of the most famous men of Europe during the first half of the nineteenth century. He was a German scholar and explorer whose interests encompassed virtually all of the natural and physical sciences. He laid the foundations for modern physical geography, geophysics, and biogeography, and helped to popularize science. His interest in Earth's geomagnetic fields led directly to the establishment of permanent observatories in British possessions around the world, one of the first instances of international scientific cooperation. Humboldt's meteorological data contributed to comparative climatology. The Humboldt Current (now called the Peru Current) off the west coast of South America was named after him.

Friedrich Wilhelm Karl Heinrich Alexander von Humboldt was born in Berlin, Germany (then Prussia), on September 14, 1769. He and his brother Wilhelm were educated at home during their early years. (Wilhelm eventually became one of Europe's most noted language scholars and educational reformers.) Alexander was at first a poor student and for some years could not decide on a career. Finally, botany stirred his interest, then geology and mineralogy. He studied at the University of Göttingen and at the School of Mines in Saxony. In 1792, he obtained a position with the Prussian government's Mining Department. He worked to improve mine safety, invented a safety lamp, and started a technical school for young miners. All the while, he was becoming convinced that his goal in life was scientific exploration.

The remainder of Humboldt's life can be divided into three segments: his expedition to South America (1799–1804); his professional life in Paris, where he organized and published the data accumulated on the expedition (1804–27); and his last years, which were spent mostly in Berlin. The first of these segments began when the Spanish government permitted him to visit Central and South America. This little-known region offered great possibilities for scientific exploration. Accompanied by the French botanist Aimé Bonpland, Humboldt covered more than 6,000 miles (9,650 kilometers) on foot, horseback, or by canoe. After the trip Humboldt went to the United States and was received by President Thomas Jefferson.

Humboldt and Bonpland returned to Europe with an immense amount of information about plants, longitude and latitude, Earth's geomagnetism, and climate. After brief visits to Berlin and a trip to Italy to inspect Mount Vesuvius, he settled in Paris readying the thirty volumes containing the results of the South American expedition.

Humboldt returned to Berlin at the insistence of the king of Prussia. He lectured on physical geography to large audiences and organized international scientific conferences. In 1829, he traveled through Russia into Siberia, as far as the Chinese frontier. His last twenty-five years were occupied chiefly with writing his *Kosmos,* one of the most ambitious scientific works ever published. In it, Humboldt presented his cosmic view of the universe as a whole. He was writing the fifth volume of this work when he died in Berlin on May 6, 1859.

toward a geographic focus on environmental and ecological studies, resource management issues, and natural hazards research.

CONCLUSION

The academic discipline of geography is extremely broad in subject matter and approaches; it contains specialists covering diverse subjects but sharing concerns over places, spaces, and environments. Indeed, the discipline is now fragmented into a substantial number of separate subcommunities among some of which there is relatively little contact. The Association of American Geographers has more than fifty separate specialty groups, for example, catering to its members' particular interests. Some physical geographers have stronger links outside their discipline than within it. The International Geographical Union—based in Rome at the "Home of Geography," provided by the Italian Geographical Society—has some two dozen commissions and about a dozen study groups.

Given this diversity of interests, encapsulating the contemporary discipline in only a small number of categories is difficult. Although the main division continues to be between physical and human geography, each field contains subdivisions and even sub-subdivisions.

One area that some have set apart from the various subdisciplinary divisions concerns the application of geographical scholarship. Geography was always applied, long before it became an identified academic discipline; much geographical knowledge was created for specific purposes. Since the discipline was established, individuals have used their knowledge in a wide range of contexts and for various

A GIS coordinator works on a high-tech wildlife "crucial habitat" mapping project to create a public resource tool now known as the Western Association of Fish and Wildlife Agencies CHAT, which aids in safeguarding wildlife in land-use planning.

types of clients. Outside of universities, some of those trained as geographers have applied their skills in a range of sectors; the US State Department had an Office of the Geographer for much of the twentieth century, for example, providing the president with daily briefings.

For the first half of the twentieth century, the development of geography as an academic discipline was closely associated with its educational role, especially in the preparation of teachers and of teaching materials. Increasingly, however, geographers responded to societal changes—especially the extending role of the state—by promoting their discipline as a potential contributor in a range of activities. The field expanded in the late twentieth century as pressures grew on universities to orient their work more to societal needs and to undertake applied research for public- and private-sector sponsors. Physical geographers' understanding of environmental processes has been directed to meet concerns over environmental issues; much public policy takes these issues into account when pursuing goals such as sustainable development. Some of these studies are relatively small-scale, such as tracing the diffusion of pollutants through water channels, identifying mineral deposits within local ecosystems, and monitoring local environmental changes and processes. Others involve larger-scale activities, such as models of climate change used to predict future ice-sheet melting, sea levels, and limits of cultivation of various plants.

Analyses from various areas of human geography were useful in many commercial applications, such as determining the best sites for facilities such as supermarkets and hospitals. Classifications of residential areas within cities were adapted to identify districts dominated by people with particular lifestyles toward which niche-market advertising could be directed; this substantial activity is widely termed geodemographics. Qualitative research findings and methods have been deployed in resolving conflicts over proposed land uses at particular sites.

Improvements made in instruments over the past 100 years or so have allowed geographers to specialize in researching geographic techniques. Satellites and spacecraft can provide geographers with images and data that enable them to determine what Earth's surface actually looks like and how it is evolving. They can analyze melting ice, keep an eye on oil spills, monitor flood damage, forecast weather, and track erosion.

The academic discipline of geography is extremely broad in subject matter and approaches; it contains specialists covering diverse subjects but sharing concerns over places, spaces, and environments. In many ways, geography as practiced today is unrecognizable from the academic discipline that was being created at the end of the nineteenth century. And yet the underlying basic concepts—of environments, spaces, and places—remain at the disciplinary core. Geography continues to illuminate major aspects of the human condition through people's interactions with their natural and social environments. The discipline was created to address issues of what is where and why. It still does just that.

GLOSSARY

adobe A type of brick made of a mixture of mud and straw that is dried by the sun.

atlas A bound collection of maps often including illustrations, informative tables, or textual matter.

cartography The science and art of making maps.

climatology The scientific study of climates.

conservation The careful use of natural resources (such as trees, oil, and so forth) to prevent them from being lost or wasted.

continent One of the great divisions of land (such as North America, South America, Europe, Asia, Africa, Australia, or Antarctica) of Earth.

ecology The study of the relatioships between living things and their environment.

equator The great circle of the celestial sphere whose plane is perpendicular to the axis of Earth.

Eurasia Landmass of Asia and Europe, chiefly used to refer to the two continents as one continent.

fossil fuel A fuel (such as coal, oil, or natural gas) that is formed from the remains of dead plants or animals.

geomorphology The scientific discipline concerned with the description and classification of Earth's topographic features.

geophysics A branch of science that deals with the physical movements and forces of Earth (such as its climate and oceans).

hydrography Of or relating to the characteristic features (as flow or depth) of bodies of water.

landform A natural feature of a land surface.

latitude Distance north or south of the equator measured in degrees up to 90 degrees.

longitude Distance measured in degrees east or west from an imaginary line (called the prime meridian) that goes from the North Pole to the South Pole and that passes through Greenwich, England.

Mercator projection A conformal map projection of which the meridians are usually drawn parallel to each other and the parallels of latitude are straight lines whose distance from each other increases with their distance from the equator.

prime meridian The meridian of 0 degrees longitude from which other longitudes are calculated.

pueblo A traditional style of dwelling of the Pueblo Indians of the southwestern United

States, typically multistoried with flat roofs and generally constructed of adobe or limestone bricks.

sedimentology A branch of science that deals with sedimentary rocks and their inclusions.

social science A particular area of study that relates to human behavior and society.

subsistence A source or means of obtaining the necessities of life.

terrestrial Relating to or occurring on Earth.

tundra A large area of flat land in northern parts of the world where there are no trees and the ground is always frozen.

urbanization The process by which towns and cities are formed and become larger as more and more people begin living and working in central areas.

volcanology A branch of science that deals with volcanic phenomena.

FOR MORE INFORMATION

American Geographical Society
32 Court Street, Suite 201
Brooklyn Heights, NY 11201
(917) 745-8354
Website: http://www.americangeo.org
The American Geographical Society aims to enhance the nation's geographic literacy and encourage sound public policy, national security, and human well-being worldwide.

Association of American Geographers
1710 16th Street NW
Washington, DC 20009-3198
(202) 234-1450
Website: http://www.aag.org
Founded in 1904, the American Association of Geographers is a nonprofit organization whose members are from more than sixty countries. The organization promotes geographical research and education and offers outreach programs for people involved in geographical studies.

The Canadian Association of Geographers
Department of Geography

McGill University
805 Sherbrooke Street West, Room 425
Montreal, QC H3A 0B9
Canada
(514) 398-4946
Website: http://www.cag-acg.ca
The Canadian Association of Geographers is the only national organization in Canada that represents practicing geographers. It promotes geographical research, and the website includes information for students who are interested in a geography career.

National Council for Geographic Education
1775 Eye Street NW, Suite 1150
Washington, DC 20006
(202) 587-5727
Website: http://www.ncge.org
Chartered in 1915, the National Council for Geographic Education encourages the teaching of geography at all levels of learning.

National Geographic Museum
1145 17th Street NW
Washington, DC 20036
(202) 857-7700

Website: http://events.nationalgeographic.com
The museum's changing exhibitions include interactive experiences and acclaimed photography displays that feature National Geographic explorations, photography, and science.

The Royal Canadian Geographical Society
1155 Lola Street, Suite 200
Ottawa, ON K1K 4C1
Canada
(613) 745-4629
Website: http://www.rcgs.org
Founded in 1929, the Royal Canadian Geographical Society strives to encourage a deeper understanding of Canada's natural, cultural, and social heritage.

Society of Woman Geographers
415 E Capitol Street SE
Washington, DC 20003
(202) 546-9228
Website: http://www.iswg.org
The Society of Woman Geographers works to "provide a medium of intellectual exchange among traveled women engaged in the study of geography and its allied arts and sciences; to further

geographical work in all its branches; to spread knowledge of the world and its people; to encourage geographical research; and to support financially fellowship programs that provide aid to outstanding women graduate students in geography and its allied fields."

Websites

Because of the changing nature of internet links, Rosen Publishing has developed an online list of websites related to the subject of this book. This site is updated regularly. Please use this link to access the list:

http://www.rosenlinks.com/SCI/geog

FOR FURTHER READING

Brotton, Jerry. *Great Maps*. New York, NY: DK Publishing, 2014.

Brotton, Jerry. *A History of the World in Twelve Maps*. New York, NY: Viking, 2013.

Dorling Kindersley. *Complete Atlas of the World*. 2nd ed. New York, NY: Dorling Kindersley Publishing, 2012.

Garfield, Simon. *On the Map: A Mind-Expanding Exploration of the Way the World Looks*. New York, NY: Gotham Books, 2013.

Heinrichs, Ann. *Gerardus Mercator: Father of Modern Mapmaking*. Minneapolis, MN: Compass Books, 2008.

Hollar, Sherman, ed. *Protecting the Environment* (The Environment: Ours to Save). New York, NY: Britannica Educational Publishing, 2012.

Imaoka, Laura. *Map. Assembling the World in an Image. Exploring the World*. London, UK: Phaidon Press, 2015.

Kaplan, Robert D. *The Revenge of Geography: What the Map Tells Us About Coming Conflicts and the Battle Against Fate*. New York, NY: Random House, 2013.

Marshall, Tim. *Prisoners of Geography: Ten Maps That Explain Everything About the World*. New York, NY: Scribner, 2015.

McPherson, Stephanie Sammartino. *Arctic Thaw: Climate Change and the Global Race for Energy Sources*. Minneapolis, MN: Twenty-first Century Books, 2015.

Pletcher, Kenneth, ed. *The Geography of China: Sacred and Historic Places* (Understanding China). New York, NY: Britannica Educational Publishing, 2011.

Pletcher, Kenneth, ed. *The Geography of India: Sacred and Historic Places* (Understanding India). New York, NY: Britannica Educational Publishing, 2011.

Rafferty, John P., ed. *Biomes and Ecosystems* (The Living Earth). New York, NY: Britannica Educational Publishing, 2011.

Rafferty, John P., ed. *Forest and Grasslands* (The Living Earth). New York, NY: Britannica Educational Publishing, 2011.

Rafferty, John P., ed. *Lakes and Wetlands* (The Living Earth). New York, NY: Britannica Educational Publishing, 2011.

Rafferty, John P., ed. *Landforms* (Geology: Landforms, Minerals, and Rocks). New York, NY: Britannica Educational Publishing, 2012.

Rafferty, John P., ed. *Oceans and Oceanography* (The Living Earth). New York, NY: Britannica Educational Publishing, 2011.

Rafferty, John P., ed. *Rivers and Streams* (The Living Earth). New York, NY: Britannica Educational Publishing, 2011.

Riffenburgh, Beau. *Mapping the World: The Story of Cartography*. London, UK: Andre Deutsch, 2015.

Woodward, John. *Geography: A Visual Encyclopedia* (Smithsonian). New York, NY: DK Publishing, 2013.

INDEX

T

U

W

Y